UNIVERSITY OF OX'
ASHMOLEAN MUSI

THE ANCIENT
NEAR EAST

P. R. S. MOOREY

ASHMOLEAN MUSEUM, OXFORD
1994

ASHMOLEAN MUSEUM PUBLICATIONS

Text & illustrations © Ashmolean Museum, Oxford 1987
All rights reserved

ISBN 0 907849 58 X

British Library Cataloguing in Publication Data

    Moorey, P.R.S.
      The Ancient Near East
      1. Middle East—Civilization
      I. Title   II. Ashmolean Museum
      939   DS56

      ISBN 0–907849–58–X

**Cover: Fragment of a hunting scene painted on a baked
clay funerary urn from Phrygia in Turkey dated to the
later fifth or fourth centuries B.C. (Ht. 32 cm; 1922.1).**

Designed by Andrew Ivett
Typeset in Bembo by Oxford Computer Typesetting, first published 1987.
Text scanned by Oxuniprint, reprinted, 1994 by Craft Print, Singapore.

1. The Legacy of the Ancient Near East and its Rediscovery

The lands of the Near (or Middle) East lie where Africa, Asia and Europe meet at the eastern end of the Mediterranean. They embrace the modern states of Iran and Iraq, of Israel and Jordan, of the Lebanon and Syria, of Saudi Arabia and the Gulf Sheikhdoms, of Turkey and the two Yemens.★ As these modern political units often have little to do with ancient cultural patterns, other terms have become current among students of antiquity, notably *Mesopotamia*, for the area between the rivers Tigris and Euphrates, embracing modern Iraq and parts of Syria; *Palestine* for the region now covered by Israel and Jordan; *Phoenicia* for the modern Lebanon, and *Anatolia* (based on the country's local name) for Turkey. In English *Persia* is also sometimes still used, following the ancient Greek, to describe Iran, whilst *Levant* broadly describes the eastern coast-lands of the Mediterranean (see map I).

The Legacy

Judaism, Christianity and Islam, three of the major religions of the World emerged here in ancient times. Today they account for most people's familiarity with the region's past. Writing, the medium through which the sacred texts of these religions survived, was invented in the area long before the texts of the Bible and the Koran took the form in which we now read

them. Thus the legacy of the ancient Near East has always been particularly closely tied to the written word.

The earliest known system of *writing*, described in its developed form as *cuneiform* (wedge-shaped) after the distinctive shape of its hundreds of characters (pl. 1), was devised by accountants specifically to write on clay tablets about 3500 B.C. in the region between the rivers Tigris and Euphrates. For over three thousand years, wherever clay tablets were used, it endured as the means of writing. Sometime between 2000 and 1500 B.C. the *idea of an alphabet* using less than thirty characters, the direct ancestor of the one we use today after transmission through the Phoenicians to the Greeks, was devised somewhere in the Levant, perhaps by Canaanites. Their system is also ancestral to the scripts of modern Arabic and Hebrew (pl. 2 and 48). Without this simple and highly effective means of record and transmission the remarkable intellectual and religious creations of the ancient Near East would have been hampered from the outset.

By recovering clay tablets through excavations, primarily in Iraq, in the last one hundred and fifty years, and by deciphering their contents, scholars have revealed many of the now dead languages and complex scribal traditions contemporary with the growth of the

★ For Egypt and Cyprus see separate Ashmolean Museum publications

Map I: The Near East.

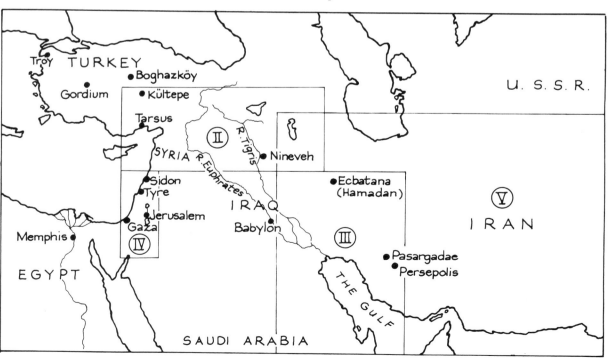

Near East: first agriculture, then town life—which appear here in developed form for the first time.

Before the end of the last ice-age (c. 8000 B.C.) hunting and gathering communities, never for long settled in one place, were starting to exploit the plants and animals which they later domesticated. Barley, emmer and einkorn wheat, with sheep, goats, pigs and cattle, were readily available in the wild state in the highland zones of modern Iran and Iraq, Turkey and the Levant, and the neighbouring rain-fed lowlands. Increasingly from the eighth millennium B.C. permanent villages flourished, supported by controlled *farming* of barley and other crops and by herding goats and sheep in some areas, cattle in others.

Yet it was another four thousand years before, in the fourth millennium B.C., concentrations of population emerged with a corporate identity, and other material features associated with *cities and civilization*. Then they did so not in the areas of rain-fed agriculture, but in southern Iraq (ancient Sumer), where the exceptional agricultural potential of restricted areas of land could only be exploited by the introduction of agricultural techniques, notably irrigation. Political institutions (high priests and kings), hierarchies of bureaucrats, and written records appeared for the first time within the towns this farming supported. Specialist crafts developed significantly under the patronage of newly emerging and wealthy palace and temple establishments. To service the craftsmen lowland agricultural surpluses were exchanged for the metals, stones and timbers, which did not occur locally, but could be

1. **Mosul marble slab from the N.W. Palace of King Assurnasirpal II (c. 883–59 B.C.) at Nimrud in Iraq carved with the figure of a bird-headed monster with a pail and pinecone; originally one of a pair flanking a sacred tree. The "standard inscription" of this king in the Assyrian language written in the cuneiform script runs across the centre. Given by Sir Henry Layard, 1850. (Ht. 2 m 32 cm; 1982.224).**

Old Testament. It no longer seems so isolated as it did to our Victorian forefathers. The diversity of the local languages and literatures of antiquity is briefly described here on pp. 45 following (see also chart II).

Until the creation of modern *science* in the age of Newton the type of scientific inquiry pursued in Europe depended wholly on a legacy from the Hellenistic period (c. 330–30 B.C.). The decipherment of inscribed cuneiform tablets from Mesopotamia has revealed that Greek scholars of this time had been influenced by earlier Babylonian studies of astronomy, mathematics and the natural world, thus endorsing the view expressed by the Greeks themselves that the Babylonians had an ancient astronomical tradition.

The invention of various writing systems and the intellectual and ideological achievement which this made possible would have been inconceivable without two even more fundamental innovations native to the

2. **Modern plaster impression of a seal of red jasper inscribed in Hebrew in a linear alphabet: "Belonging to Miqneyahu son of Yehokal"; seventh century B.C. (14 × 12 × 7 mm; 1943.2).**

3. Reverse of a clay tablet from Iraq inscribed with Greek letters in the mid-second century B.C. So far the language involved is not certainly identified, as it is not Greek and appears not to be Akkadian (or Sumerian); it might be in a dialect of Aramaic or merely an incoherent scribal exercise in writing Greek letters. (8.2 × 6 cm; 1937.993).

The Rediscovery of the Ancient Near East

Since the early Christian era pilgrimage had always taken the pious, the curious, and the intrepid from Europe to the Near East; but the journey was rigorous and long remained so. When Chaucer recorded that the Wife of Bath had been three times to Jerusalem he gave full measure of that remarkable woman. By the sixteenth century merchants and envoys, scholars and travellers had begun to replace the wandering men and women of the church, though the Bible was long to remain the guiding light and inspiration for travel and study. In fascinating books they recounted their journeys with varying degrees of accuracy, since anecdotes rather than careful observation characterized them until the eighteenth century was well advanced. By the early nineteenth century critical scientific study had begun to supersede ill-disciplined, if informed, curiosity and the necessary basis of accurate topography and historical geography began to be laid for future archaeological research. Not only standing ruins excited interest. At an early date it was realized that the many artificial mounds (or *tells/tepes*) of the region marked the sites of abandoned ancient settlements.

obtained from the adjacent highlands of Iran and Turkey.

In a previous generation it was widely believed that many cultural and technological innovations first evolved in the Near East were diffused westwards into the Mediterranean and Europe, profoundly influencing local populations at less advanced stages of political, social or economic development. In the last twenty years there has been a powerful reaction against diffusion as an explanation of cultural change. Scholars have, in many instances, rejected links with the east in favour of local, autonomous growth largely independent of foreign stimuli. Both extreme explanations are too simplistic. In the Near East and in Europe complex and diverse factors were at work. Possibilities inherent in existing ways-of-life were realised under various stimuli, some from distant sources, some from nearer home, some from within, as circumstances changed. At all times developing communities were side-by-side with older, more fully developed societies with whom they were in regular contact; such interrelationships encouraged the transfer of ideas as much as the exchange of commodities.

After the campaigns of Alexander the Great (c. 330–323 B.C.) the Near East was steadily transformed by fresh and dynamic forces. New political, social and economic systems emerged. Cultural life was profoundly transformed as Aramaic and Greek, written in linear alphabets (pl. 3), and their own intellectual traditions steadily superseded the older languages and literatures predominantly written in cuneiform. With their disappearance the ancient culture of the Near East was largely eclipsed by the first century A.D.

4. Stone altar from Palmyra in Syria inscribed in the local language; it is dated in September A.D. 85 and shows an incense altar (*hamman*) between the two figures. It was given to the University of Oxford in the eighteenth century. (Ht. 48 cm; C.2–9).

The pioneer excavators in the region were a curious mixture of European and American diplomats and gentleman-scholars, soldiers and administrators, often fired as much by national pride and a desire to fill museum cases with "treasures" in their own countries, as by a quest for knowledge. Their achievements were spectacular and a remarkable generation of excavators and linguists in the middle decades of the nineteenth century changed for ever our understanding of the biblical world. Exciting accounts written for the general reading public ensured wide interest and enduring support for new research.

In *Mesopotamia* (modern Iraq and northern Syria) attention was first concentrated on the great palaces of the Assyrian kings with Botta digging for the French at Khorsabad and Nineveh, Layard and his successor Rassam at Nimrud and Nineveh for the British from the 1840s (pl. 5). These excavations revealed to an astonished world the magnificent sculptured stone reliefs lining palace walls and the vast library of cuneiform tablets assembled for King Assurbanipal (c. 668–27 B.C.) at Nineveh. In time all the major western powers had established themselves with centres of research in what was then part of the Ottoman Empire ruled from Istanbul: the French at Telloh (from 1877), the Americans at Nippur (from 1889), the Germans at Assur (from 1903) and at Babylon (from 1899), and the British intermittently at various sites. Between the World Wars the pattern changed little until the Kingdom of Iraq emerged, though methods were steadily refined. Work was largely in the hands of Anglo-American expeditions at Kish and Ur; of the Americans in the Diyala Valley; of the Germans at Uruk; and of the French at Larsa and Mari, to name but the largest expeditions.

An Englishman, William Loftus, excavated briefly at Susa in *Iran* in 1851 and in 1853; but not until 1884 did the French arrive there to begin a series of excavations that continued until the recent Iranian revolution. From 1884 to the 1930s virtually no expatriate archaeologists other than the French worked in Iran, which remained largely closed to foreign exploration. In the decade before 1940 American expeditions to Tepe Hissar in northeast Iran, to Persepolis and into Luristan, and French expeditions at Tepe Giyan and Tepe Sialk, as well as at Susa, threw isolated and random shafts of light on the development of Iran from earliest times to the Achaemenid period (c. 550–330 B.C.). As early as 1904 the American scholar Pumpelly had initiated archaeological explorations in Turkestan (Anau) that anticipated in a remarkable way many of the field methods and attitudes not otherwise brought to the Near East until after 1945.

Syria and Palestine, the biblical heartlands, were, and long remained, a special case. The enormous public response to Layard's work stimulated interest in the archaeology of Palestine leading to the creation of the Palestine Exploration Fund in England in 1865 and to its spectacular, if dangerous, excavations in Jerusalem from 1867–70. This work was done by Royal Engineers directed by Captain Warren, who was memorably concise in describing his methods: "The system adopted in excavating at Jerusalem was that ordinarily used in military mining; therefore it is unnecessary to describe the details . . ."

In 1890 the famous Egyptologist Flinders Petrie demonstrated, by cutting a vertical section through the ancient settlement mound at Tell el-Hesi, that each main period of occupation had distinctive types of pottery. By correlating this relative sequence with Egyptian seals and rare inscriptions he worked out an absolute chronology. His scheme has been constantly modified, but never fundamentally altered. This brief excavation was a precocious demonstration of the fundamental role of stratigraphy, typology and cross-dating (cf. p. 8) in the archaeology of the Near East. But its implications were lost for at least a generation when Petrie returned to work in Egypt.

The pattern thereafter in Syro-Palestine was much as in Mesopotamia, with an emphasis on recovering architecture, inscribed objects and works of art, often in pursuit of biblical history rather than general cultural history, at sites like Gezer, Jericho, Jerusalem, Megiddo and Taanach (see pp. 30–32).

Significant new trends emerged in Reisner's and then in Kenyon's analysis of the stratigraphy of Samaria (1909–10; 1931–5), Albright's attention to pottery typology at Tell Beit Mirsim (1926–32), and the excavations in prehistoric caves by Turville-Petre (1925) and Dorothy Garrod (1928–34). In Syria excavations by the French at Ras Shamra (Ugarit), the Danes at Hama, the British at Tell Atchana (Alalakh), Brak and Chagar Bazar and the Americans on *tells* in the Amuq region steadily began to reveal the cultural history and foreign contacts, as well as the remarkable prehistory, of that area.

Although the standing ruins of Hellenistic and Roman cities in *Turkey* (Anatolia) had long called attention to that country's antiquities, the advent of serious excavation there is for ever associated with one of archaeology's epic tales. Schliemann's excavations from 1870 at Hissarlik, in northwest Turkey, which he identified with Homeric Troy, were as momentous in

5. Fragmentary Mosul marble slab from the N.W. Palace of King Assurnasirpal II (c. 883–59 B.C.) at Nimrud in Iraq showing a bird-headed monster. It originally belonged to Lady Layard, who received it from her husband, Sir Henry Layard, who excavated it. (Ht. 72 cm; 1950.241). Compare plate 1 here).

their own way as the work of Layard and Botta a generation earlier in Mesopotamia. However, the mainstream peoples of ancient Anatolia were first investigated on sites in Eastern Turkey like Carchemish (Djerablus) and Van, at the centre of ancient Urartu (p. 36). From 1906 German excavations at the Hittite capital of Boghazköy have played a crucial part until today in revealing the major archives of tablets so far found in Turkey. However, through the 1920s and 1930s, sites like Alishar, Alaça Hüyük, Kültepe (Karum Kanesh), Kusura, Mersin and Tarsus, and Troy again, were opened up by Turkish and foreign archaeologists to reveal the immensely varied and regionally distinctive cultures of pre- and post-Hittite Turkey (see pp. 32–36).

Since 1945 excavations have proliferated in the Near East as national departments of antiquities have flourished, local schools of archaeology have emerged and with them policies for nurturing contacts with foreign colleagues and for fostering international co-operation in field research. Whole new areas, in Iran and Afghanistan, in Saudi Arabia and in the Gulf, have been added to the archaeological map, whilst the most significant advances in archaeological field-research strategies and in thinking about processes of cultural change have arisen in the study of prehistoric societies.

The pioneers tended to work alone or with very small teams of architects and philologists; the post-World War II generations have increasingly operated as teams, encompassing ever wider ranges of speciality in both humane and scientific studies. The best research has been focussed on specific problems, with research teams which offer a wide range of expertise. Braidwood's seminal expedition to Iraqi Kurdistan from 1948 in quest of early farming communities or,

more recently, the research on early metal exploitation at Timna in Israel and in Oman, are good examples of this approach.

The "Wheeler-Kenyon" technique of stratigraphical digging and analysis, used at Jericho (1952–8) (pl. 6), improved excavation methods in a fundamental way, though it was steadily modified by its critics to take account of wide horizontal exposures and the varying conditions of mound formation found across the Near East. Surveys to date sites by the distinctive pottery sherds found on the surface, combined with selective excavation, are now commonplace. This approach is part of a trend in which mounds (*tells* or *tepes*) are seen as part of a landscape, in all its geographical and historical complexity. The pace of modern development, notably the erection of dams on major rivers, has opened whole areas to intensive, systematic investigation through survey and excavation before flooding. But still chance plays its hand and outstanding discoveries like the Neolithic settlement at Çatal Hüyük in Turkey (p. 18) or the third millennium archives from Tell Mardikh (Ebla) in Syria (p. 49) continue to surprise.

The explanatory tools of archaeology were largely adopted from geology and ethnography in the nineteenth century as much as from history and anthropology. Today the latest aims and methods of the natural and social sciences, not least quantitative techniques, have been introduced to modify continuously both the explanatory models and the procedures used by archaeologists to recover and process their data. Of all the regions in the world where archaeology is intensively pursued the Near East remains the one where the most traditional and the most radical methods may be seen in operation, often side-by-side. This, combined with its fundamental importance to the development of so many aspects of our own civilization, makes its study one of continuing interest and intellectual excitement.

6. Simplified drawing of the stratigraphy (see p. 9) of the mound at Jericho as revealed in Trench I of the Kenyon excavations (1952–58).

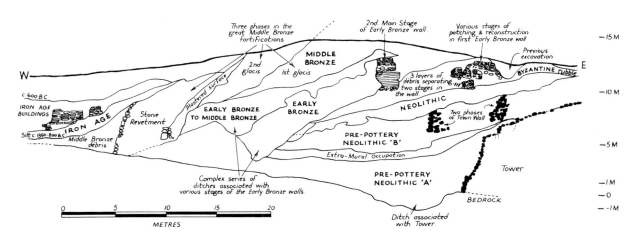

Tells and Time

The sequence of human settlement in the Near East before about 3000 B.C. is inferred almost entirely from superimposed debris in ancient settlement mounds: *tells*. Supplementary information from surface surveys is useful only in so far as it may be tied into a basic sequence. Buildings of mud, mud-brick or rubble, with plastered walls and roofs of light timber, mud and rushmats, when they collapse, leave little or nothing to salvage and the newcomer will merely level off the ruins and build above them. In the course of time this accumulating debris forms a mound in which the sequence of remains can be observed and recorded by cutting trenches into it (compare pl. 6).

Through *Stratigraphy* (observing variations in a

7. Outer: cornelian necklace from Tell Farah (South), Israel, c. 1300 B.C.; inner, lapis lazuli, cornelian and etched cornelian necklace from Kish, Iraq, c. 2500 B.C. (1930.546; 1925.261).

mound's growth) one can place changes in architecture, techniques (potting, metalworking, etc.) and domestic equipment in order of time and relate them to observed interruptions or changes of settlement. Distinctive types of pottery, less commonly of other small objects, allow for the correlation of levels in one mound with those in others. The proper study of materials like bones, seeds and other organic matter, previously ignored, now increasingly permits a much greater understanding of the ancient landscape so that *tells* are seen as parts of a human settlement pattern rather than as isolated "sites".

B.C.	TURKEY	SYRO-PALESTINE	IRAQ	IRAN	B.C.
9000	FINAL PALAEOLITHIC : Hunting & collecting	(Natufian) cereal collecting			9000
8000		PRE-POTTERY NEOLITHIC (PPN 'A')	↙ Beginning of farming PRE-POTTERY NEOLITHIC		8000
7000	PRE-POTTERY NEOLITHIC (Basal Hacilar)	(PPN 'B')		EARLY NEOLITHIC	7000
6000	POTTERY NEOLITHIC (Catal Hüyük) EARLY CHALCOLITHIC (Upper Hacilar)	POTTERY NEOLITHIC (PN 'A') (PN 'B')	POTTERY NEOLITHIC EARLY CHALCOLITHIC (Halaf)		6000
5000				LATE NEOLITHIC	5000
	LATE CHALCOLITHIC	CHALCOLITHIC (Ghassulian)	LATE CHALCOLITHIC (Ubaid)		
4000	(transition)	(transition)	(Uruk IV) PROTOLITERATE	CHALCOLITHIC	4000
	EARLY BRONZE AGE EB I	PROTO-URBAN EARLY BRONZE AGE EB I	(Jamdat Nasr) = Uruk III)		
3000	EB II	EB II	I		3000
	EB III	EB III	EARLY DYNASTIC II III	EARLY BRONZE AGE	
	EB IV	EB IV (EB/MB)	AKKADIAN UR III ISIN-LARSA		
2000	MIDDLE BRONZE AGE Assyrian Colony Period HITTITE OLD KINGDOM	MIDDLE BRONZE AGE MB I MB II	OLD ASSYRIAN / OLD BABYLONIAN (Amorite)	(Old Elamite) LATE BRONZE AGE	2000
	(LATE BRONZE AGE) HITTITE NEW EMPIRE	LATE BRONZE AGE LB I LB II	KASSITE/ MITANNIAN MIDDLE ASSYRIAN AND BABYLONIAN	(Middle Elamite) IRON I	
1000	(IRON AGE) PHRYGIAN/NEO-HITTITE LYDIAN ACHAEMENID (Persian)	IRON AGE IRON I (ISRAEL, JUDAH, PHOENICIA) IRON II IRON III ACHAEMENID (Persian)	NEO-ASSYRIAN NEO-BABYLONIAN ACHAEMENID (Persian)	(Neo-Elamite) IRON II IRON III ACHAEMENID	1000

Left margin (rotated millennium labels): 9TH MILL. · 8TH MILL. · 7TH MILL. · 6TH MILL. · FIFTH MILLENNIUM B.C. · FOURTH MILLENNIUM B.C. · THIRD MILLENNIUM B.C. · SECOND MILLENNIUM B.C. · 1ST MILLENNIUM B.C.

Chart I: Chronological Table.

For geographical and political reasons prehistoric research in the Near East has progressed at an uneven pace. The standard terms are *Neolithic*, *Chalcolithic* and *Bronze Ages*, which broadly signify technological stages, but they have never been systematically applied. Where they have, such terms as "Pre-pottery" or "Aceramic" Neolithic have crept in to describe the earlier phases of the Neolithic. In Turkey and Syro-Palestine, very broadly speaking, this system has been followed. In Iraq and Iran a relative prehistoric chronology has commonly been denoted by 'phases' or 'cultures', as in Egypt, named after the archaeological site at which they were first recognized. Occasionally they overlap in time to some extent as with the Hassuna, Samarra and Halaf cultures of Iraq and northern Syria (see chart I).

Measurements of residual radioactivity in ancient carbon (*Carbon-14 dating*) has only recently been applied in a systematic fashion in this region. This method, despite its acknowledged uncertainties, and the cavalier way in which such dates have often been used, increasingly provides a basic framework for ordering the complex and differential development of human societies in Near Eastern prehistory. Although the first appearance of writing, in the Uruk IV period in Iraq, c. 3500–3200 B.C., is conventionally taken to distinguish *prehistory* from *history*, there is an interval, varying considerably in length from region to region, before the recording of events and personalities may be described in any sense as historic. This is true in a very basic way for Egypt★ and Mesopotamia, starting at different points in the first half of the third millennium B.C. Their absolute chronologies form the basic framework for the area. From about 2500 B.C. it becomes possible to correlate, if only tentatively, archaeological evidence, contemporary inscriptions, and an absolute chronology calculated with the assistance of local king-lists and isolated astronomical observations (see pp. 23 ff.).

The Assyrians and Babylonians had no fixed chronological framework comparable to our dating by years of the Christian Era (A.D.) until the Greek rulers (Seleucids) fixed the first year of King Seleucus I (reckoned at Babylon from April 3rd, 311 B.C.) as the basis for such a system (*Anno Seleucidarum*: A.S.: Seleucid Era). Before then, from about 2350 B.C., time had been officially measured year by year in one of three main ways: by identifying the year through important events; by referring directly to the number of a regnal year; or by describing the year with the name of a high ranking official: what is known as the *limmu* or eponym system in Assyria (pl. 8).

The practical value of such dating systems over a period of time obviously depended upon the existence

★ See the Ashmolean handbook *Ancient Egypt* (1983), 10–15.

8. Modern plaster impression from an agate cylinder seal of Nabu-shar-usur, *limmu* official in 786 B.C. during the reign of King Adadnirari III of Assyria. It shows a man and woman, probably the seal's owner and his wife, before a seated goddess and deity symbols. (Ht. 35 mm; 1922.61).

9. Baked clay prism ("Weld-Blundell Prism") inscribed in the cuneiform script with the most important copy of the Sumerian King List giving rulers from "before the Flood" to King Sin-magir of Isin (c. 1827–17 B.C.). Probably written at Larsa in Iraq. (Ht. 20 cm; 1923.444).

of comprehensive and interrelated lists for the year-names, for royal dynasties (groups of kings) with the length of each reign, and for successive dynasties. Such lists, inscribed on clay tablets and prisms (pl. 9) have survived; but they vary in time-range, are not always complete and do not always indicate dynastic interruptions and overlaps. In the earliest periods, particularly, the compilers were more interested in the sequence of events than in the intervals between them, so the figures cited have to be treated with caution.

Transposing such ancient lists, with their gaps and scribal errors, into a continuous sequence with royal dates expressed in years B.C. is a complicated task. There are still major points of uncertainty. An almost completely preserved Assyrian king-list takes the sequence back to the fourteenth century B.C., when there are direct correlations with the Amarna Period in Egypt (the time of Akhnaten and Tutankhamum), within a margin of error of a generation or so. These Assyrian lists may be broadly correlated with contemporary Babylonian records.

Earlier, where for a crucial interval records fail us,

the margin of error in calculating absolute dates rises sharply. In the first half of the second millennium B.C. is to be found the most crucial unresolved problem in the historical chronology of Babylonia. The absolute dating of the end of the First Dynasty of Babylon, to which the famous King Hammurabi of Babylon belongs, depends upon records of astronomical events that are partial and faulty in transmission. Consequently the Dynasty is "floating" over a period of about one and a half centuries. The revised *Cambridge Ancient History*—and many standard works of reference—have adopted for convenience the so-called "Middle Chronology" placing this dynasty c. 1894–1595 B.C. However, on the latest calculations the "High Chronology" c. 1950–1651 B.C. is more probable. The "Low Chronology" c. 1830–1531 B.C., if less favoured, may not yet be ruled out. King-lists, year-names and occasional synchronisms allow for a plausible reconstruction of absolute chronology back another five hundred years from the beginning of the First Dynasty of Babylon, whatever date that is given.

The chronological systems of Egypt on the one hand, Mesopotamia on the other, frame all accounts of early Near Eastern history. In the second millennium B.C. king-lists may to some extent be reconstructed for the Hittites in Turkey and the Mitannian rulers in Syria; but they have to be cross-referenced to Egypt or Mesopotamia for absolute dating (see chart I).

10. **Two burnished baked clay vessels in the shape of zebus (bulls) from the region of N.W. Iran popularly known as "Amlash"; c. 1400–1000 B.C. The authenticity of these vessels has been established by thermoluminescence tests. (Ht. 39 cm; 1964.347–8).**

In the first millennium B.C. the Old Testament offers the basis for calculation of an independent absolute chronology of the Kings of Israel and Judah; but even this is not "fixed", despite occasional correlations with Egypt and Mesopotamia. The chronology of the kings of Israel was calculated on the basis of that of the kings of Judah and *vice versa*. In the absence of modern knowledge of the starting date or the criteria

11. Fragment of a Mosul marble relief from the S.W. Palace of King Sennacherib (c. 704–681 B.C.) at Nineveh in Iraq, probably showing an episode in his Babylonian campaign (cf. the date palms); the woman and child riding on a mule are captives escorted by Assyrian soldiers. (Ht. 92 cm; 1933.1575).

used many solutions have been proposed, some differing only by a few years; but general agreement is only reached with the reign of Josiah (c. 640/39–609 B.C.).

2. A Diversity of Peoples

Peoples in a landscape

The Near East until modern times was characterized by widely dispersed pockets of intensive settlement in an otherwise semi-arid landscape that was largely inhospitable to settled communities. Where they flourished, there were recurrent shared features: water was constant, abundant and relatively accessible; the extremes of heat in summer were not matched by such extremes of winter cold; the soil was rich enough for cultivation and communications by land or water were relatively easy. A defensive facility was often a vital subsidiary

consideration. These concentrations of people were not isolated. They were linked by broad areas across which long-distance movement by pastoralists was possible and by trade contacts with peripheral regions that provided vital resources. The hazards of subsistence (for the lives of most ancient peoples were ultimately rural lives to a degree now hard to appreciate) drew the settled and the mobile into a relationship in which complementary cereal cultivation and animal husbandry often sustained patterns of settlement that would otherwise have been much more vulnerable.

12. **Fragment of a Mosul marble relief from the S.W. Palace of King Sennacherib (c. 704–681 B.C.) at Nineveh in Iraq showing an Assyrian soldier leading a horse with harnessing typical of the period. (Ht. 34 cm; 1950.240).**

The famous balance and interaction of "the desert and the sown" is indeed at the heart of the region's history.

Intimately linked with this relationship were two other persistent traits of ancient Near Eastern life. First, cities exercised lasting control over distant hinterlands, particularly in Iran; and second, trading patterns went unchanged for millennia together with recurrent cultural interactions through the overland transport that linked distant regions. Goods were carried first on the backs of men, then of asses, and by the earlier first millennium B.C. increasingly of camels (pls. 10–12). In this landscape the wheel and the boat always played restricted roles. This communications network proved so effective that it encompassed remarkable distances and was so resilient that it was largely resistant in the long run to changing political circumstances.

Thus across the region—formidable as the barriers were—town and country, desert and sown, centre and periphery, were inextricably linked as commodities and ideas constantly passed backwards and forwards across traditional boundaries and enduring rivalries.

Nomadic and semi–nomadic peoples regularly interacted with settled populations, sometimes mutually supportive, sometimes hostilely disruptive. It is this pattern that underlies the following section as it offers a bird's eye view of nearly eight millennia in the Near East.

From time immemorial the population of the Near East has been unusually diverse and fluid; but it is only those people who have left traces in contemporary written records that generally emerge in modern studies with names (chart II). It needs always to be remembered that such apparently ethnic terms as "Akkadians" or "Hurrians" are commonly used as short-hand for "Akkadian-speaking peoples" etc., categorized by scholars in a way they would not themselves necessarily have recognized as significant. As the modern history of the region makes so painfully apparent, people here have always imposed as many restrictions on one another as the formidable landscape does on them all. Such human constraints were born of diverse and kaleidoscopic differences in political allegiance, in ideological preferences, in basic patterns of social behaviour, and in languages (see chart II and pp. 45 ff.).

Chart II: Diagram of the Timespans of the Written Evidence for the Main Languages of the Ancient Near East.

14

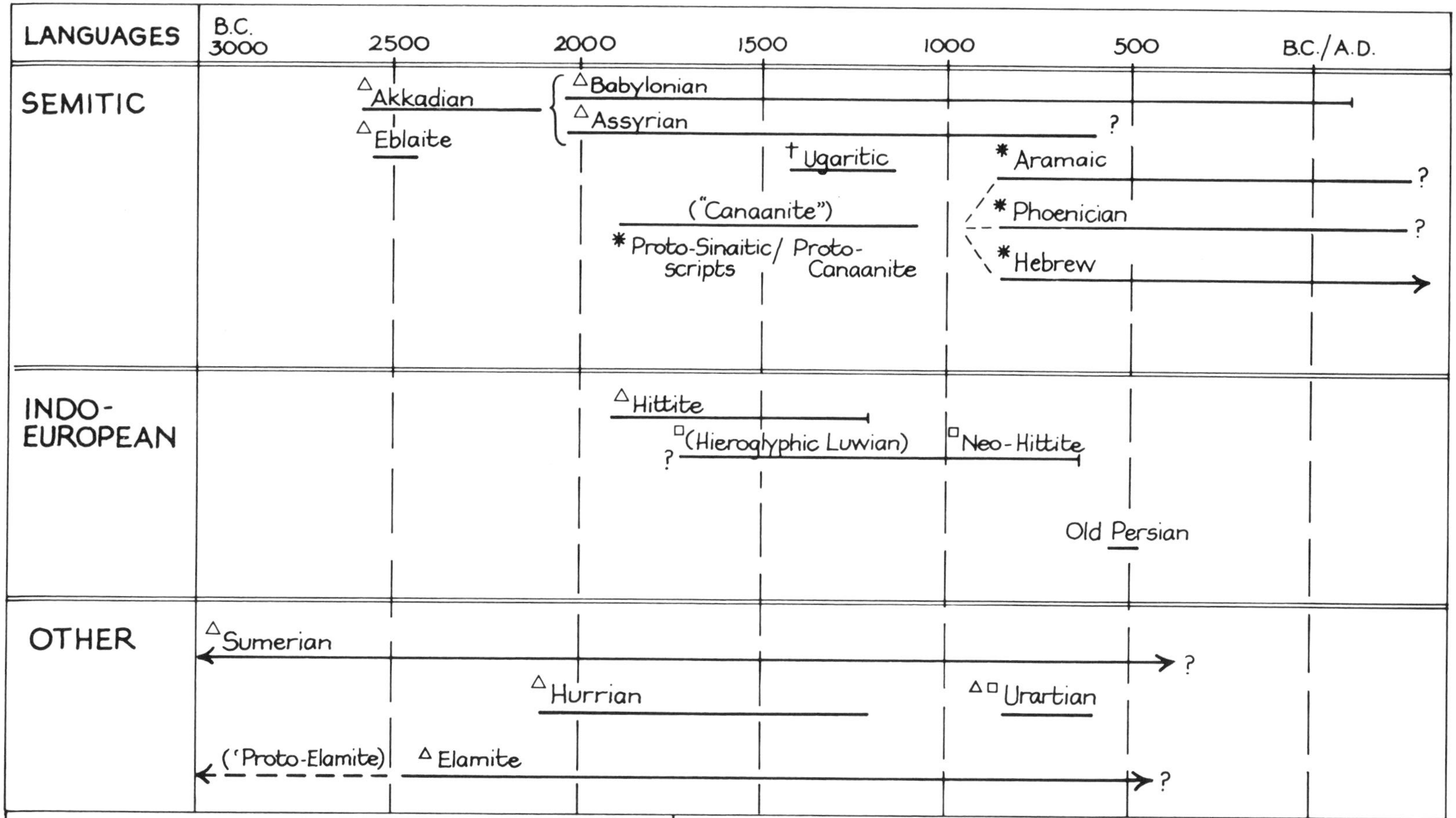

LANGUAGES	B.C. 3000	2500	2000	1500	1000	500	B.C./A.D.

SEMITIC

△ Akkadian
△ Eblaite
{ △ Babylonian / △ Assyrian } ?
† Ugaritic
("Canaanite")
* Proto-Sinaitic / Proto-Canaanite scripts ?
* Aramaic ?
* Phoenician ?
* Hebrew

INDO-EUROPEAN

△ Hittite
□ (Hieroglyphic Luwian) ?
□ Neo-Hittite
Old Persian

OTHER

△ Sumerian
△ Hurrian
△ □ Urartian ?
△ Elamite
('Proto-Elamite') ?

N.B. ① In *Iraq* it is assumed that the pictographic script of Uruk IV-III (c. 3500-3000 B.C.) was used to write the Sumerian language.
② In *Iran* Elamite was preceded by the undeciphered 'Proto-Elamite' and 'Linear Elamite' scripts.

KEY:
△   cuneiform scripts.
+   alphabetic scripts in wedge-shaped signs.
*   alphabetic scripts in linear signs.
□   local hieroglyphic scripts.

13. Upper part of a plastered skull from Jericho with eyes inlaid with cowrie shells set horizontally. This may be a deliberate attempt to capture the likeness of a particular person as they are usually set vertically; Pre-Pottery Neolithic B, c. 7000 B.C. (Ht. 15.2 cm; 1955.565).

In a sketch as brief as this there is no room for descriptions of landscape and the distribution of natural resources; for that the reader is referred to books cited in the first part of the bibliography on p. 55. Two general points must, however, be made.

First, it is now widely accepted that from about 8000 B.C. overall climatic conditions in the Near East were much as they are today. But this is a region in which even marginal variation in annual rainfall can have the most devastating effects on animals, men and vegetation. It is this critical level that, at present, eludes the modern investigator, though its potentially disruptive effects must always be borne in mind.

Second, in many parts of the area the activities of men have transformed the landscape. Wide areas that were once densely forested and fertile are now barren and wasted. The ancient appearance of the landscape may not then be assumed, it has to be demonstrated. Many current research programmes are directed to this end.

The Peoples of Prehistory c. 10,000–3000 B.C.

The shift from widely scattered, relatively small and mobile bands of hunter-gatherers, seasonally camping, to more concentrated communities of settled farmers, cultivating crops and raising animals, is universally regarded as a major turning-point in the development of human societies. So also is the subsequent emergence of concentrations of population in towns, variously distinguished by a more complex social organization, by walls, and by monumental public buildings. The Near East has always had a special interest for students of antiquity as the region where it is possible to study both these crucial transitions at their earliest known appearance.

A number of basic features were to prove critical in the region's development in prehistory: areas highly suitable for intensive cultivation set between desert, mountain and steppe; local plants and animals suitable for controlled cultivation and husbandry; rivers with a steady flow of water to facilitate irrigation; and accessible (if at times distant) supplies of useful or desirable minerals to be obtained only through travel and trade. All contributed in their way to the multiplicity of factors that stimulated social and cultural developments of unusual interest between about 8000 and 2000 B.C.

Hunting (see cover picture)

Although presented here, for convenience of description, as a sequence, it has always to be remembered that Near Eastern society throughout antiquity was a mosaic once villages and towns emerged, with peripheral semi-nomadic communities, who continued to exploit wild resources, plant and animal, as and when they chose. Hunting was always to remain a necessity both to supplement diet and to counteract predators. It became, moreover, in time a pastime for the privileged and wealthy through which they improved and displayed their skills with weapons, in driving horses and

14. Baked clay model of a one-humped camel loaded with two pigs; made in Syria in the Roman Period. (Ht. 10.5 cm; 1956.1045).

15. Two pottery vessels from Hacilar in Turkey, c. 5500 B.C. The authenticity of these vessels has been established by a thermo–luminescence test. (Ht. 9.8 cm; 1971.929; Ht. 12 cm; 1971.930).

chariots (pl. 20), and in riding; they schooled themselves for war as they hunted. In religious imagery success in the chase became a potent metaphor for man's persistent struggle to master the untamed and unpredictable forces of nature. As a hunter the ruler proved his strength, sometimes in carefully staged exhibitions, and epitomized the aspirations of his aristocracy.

Farming and the earliest permanent settlements

In the Epipalaeolithic (*Natufian*) Period c. 12,000–8000 B.C., sickles of flint and grinding stones had been developed to process edible seeds. These were the tools vital to eventual full-scale use of ripe cereal crops, but it is not certain at this stage how far they were under controlled cultivation. At certain places, like Abu Hureyra in Syria, where a wild cereal harvest could be obtained, semi-permanent base camps grew up.

Throughout the Near East as a whole after 8000 B.C. there was a steadily growing degree of settlement for the first time in small villages in favourable locations, though initially without any indication of domesticated livestock (*Pre-Pottery Neolithic A*). It

seems likely that at this time cereals (barley and wheat) and vegetables, plants adapted to a Mediterranean climate with its summer drought, were domesticated by people hunting the relatively sparse game in the arid lands of the Levant and continuing to collect other species of wild plants as they had for millennia.

The regular husbandry of domesticated animals may have been a separate process that was only slowly grafted on to cereal farming. Goats, and perhaps sheep, the first preferred domestic animals, may have come under systematic control by man in regions other than those where the earliest cereal farming was practised. By the later ninth millennium the Zagros mountains of Iran were an early centre of goat domestication; at much the same time sheep may have been herded in the Zagros foothills. It is possible that in the Zagros the use of herds was still greater than in the Levant long after effective agriculture was commonplace in the Near East. Domesticated cattle appear by the early seventh millennium B.C. in Turkey. At about the same time (*Pre-Pottery Neolithic B*), goats alone were introduced into the farming settlements of Syro-Palestine.

From about 7000–5000 B.C. permanent village life, supported by a combination of herding and mixed farming, was widely practised. Culturally the patterns varied from the outset and archaeology only throws concentrated shafts of light on the outstanding differences. In the earlier Neolithic, before the use of pottery, *Jericho* (10 acres) has striking features. It is

17

16. **Baked clay female fertility figurine decorated with red paint, originally sitting on a low stool (perhaps the position adopted for child-birth); from Chagar Bazar in Syria, c. 5500 B.C. (Ht. 10 cm; 1936.90).**

remarkable for its stone wall, with at least one tower rising to a height of eight metres, within a ditch. Artistic expression in the service of unknown ideologies is also evident in the reconstruction of facial features with plaster, paint and inlaid eyes on detached human skulls and in large, formalized human figures of plaster over organic or clay cores (pl. 13).

From an early date obsidian from sources in Anatolia was exchanged in semi-finished form as prepared cores for blade tools in a network of contact extending deep into southern Israel, to the Gulf and far into Iran. Colourful ornamental stones like turquoise, from Sinai and from Iran, shells from the Red Sea or the Gulf, jadeite, serpentine and greenstone from the Taurus mountains in Turkey, travelled equally widely. It is assumed that domesticated seeds and animals, and relevant information, travelled along the same routes explaining why major innovations in farming and craft skills appear at much the same time over the whole area.

As Jericho stands out in the earlier Neolithic so does *Çatal Hüyük* in Turkey in the later (c. 6300–5400 B.C.). It is the largest Neolithic farming village yet known, at over 30 acres, with a remarkable level of material culture in the very small area so far excavated. Rectangular houses of timber and mudbrick were built like a honeycomb and entered from the roof. About a third of the excavated structures, the "shrines", had wall paintings (as did the houses) and plaster reliefs of animals and human figures. The material culture was rich in range and quality. Pottery had now appeared, its origins perhaps to be found in the white plasterware of earlier sites in Syria. Fine bone and obsidian tools, ornaments of smelted copper and lead, wooden boxes and vessels, woven textiles, baskets and leather goods and a varied repertory of stone and terracotta figurines distinguish this site. Later developments of the same cultural tradition at *Hacilar*, farther west in Turkey, c. 5600–4900 B.C., are characterized by a remarkable pottery industry, notable for its painted decoration and anthropomorphic vessels (pl. 15).

From about 6000 B.C. attention shifts to the lands east of the Euphrates, to the river valley of Mesopotamia where, about two thousand years later, urban civilization emerged in what was to be known in historic times as Sumer and in its eastern neighbour modern Khuzistan in southwest Iran, round the site of Susa.

The earliest farmers had concentrated in regions where seasonally moist soil required minimal preparation for cultivation with hoes and other hafted stone tools. Along rivers crossing the North Mesopotamian plain, for instance, village settlements of the Halaf Culture, c. 6000–5000 B.C., already had trinkets in base metals, clearly distinguished areas for pottery manufacture, communal storage facilities, and a variety of fertility figurines (pl. 16). Expansion beyond these restricted zones is evident in the sixth millennium B.C. In lowland Mesopotamia farmers of the "Samarra Culture" pioneered simple irrigation techniques on or beyond the present 200 metre isohyet, as at *Choga Mami*. At the same time farmers of the "Hassuna Culture" exploited the steppe of Northern Mesopotamia within the 200 metre isohyet, where rainfall was usually sufficient, though greater soil preparation may have been necessary for growing cereal crops.* It is likely that it was in this region that man first harnessed animal power to his service by yoking cattle in pairs to pull simple ploughs (pl. 17). The combination of plough and basic irrigation techniques allowed for major expansion of agriculture in the Ubaid Period, c. 4500–3500 B.C., in the alluvial plain of Mesopotamia, now increasingly capable of supporting substantial populations.

Already at Choga Mami, close to the Zagros in Iran, and at Tell es-Sawwan on the central Tigris, settlements of the "Samarra Culture", c. 5500–5000 B.C., had defensive walls with a degree of planning both in the layout of the settlements and in individual rectilinear mudbrick houses, perhaps the homes of extended families. This indicates a degree of community organization, whilst differences in the richness of grave furnishings show emerging social stratification. It is likely that the networks of exchange and contact long used for obsidian and other minerals were now steadily exploited to bring in from the highland periphery the greater quantities of metal, stone and wood required by the emerging ruling groups in lowland communities. Such supplies, when not brought by water, were now probably more often carried on the backs of donkeys than of men. The appearance of stone stamp seals and clay sealings on consignments of goods and storeroom locks implies property ownership and possibly central redistributive agencies for goods within the major settlements (pl. 18).

The emergence of towns

A town may simply be defined for present purposes as a concentration of people linked in corporate relationship who were settled in one place, with a substantial proportion of the population engaged full-time in non-agricultural pursuits, such as administration, manufacturing, temple and cult maintenance, business and trade. Thus a town was distinguished from settlements in which the vast majority of inhabitants were still engaged in food production for subsistence, although many of its citizens might still be intimately associated with the agricultural hinterland that sustained every town. In Iraq, from remote prehistory, there seems to

* *Isohyet:* line on a map connecting two or more places with the same amount of rainfall.

17. Modern plaster impression from a stone cylinder seal made in Syria, c. 3000 B.C., showing a man with a simple plough; birds, animals and a scorpion in the surrounding area. (27 × 24 mm; 1909.1137).

18. Stone stamp seals with animal-shaped backs from Mesopotamia and one of the earliest type of cylinder seals, with a recumbent silver ram as its handle. The stamp seals are carved with crude animal designs, but the cylinder has an elaborate scene of cows and calves illustrating farming activities in southern Iraq, c. 3500–3000 B.C. (Cylinder: Ht. 53 mm; 1964.744; Stamps: 1890.81, 1920.257–8, 1924.57).

have been a steadily evolving sense of corporate religion; each settlement had a patron god or goddess and at least one temple to that deity. In towns differential access to power in terms of economic and political resources was much more marked than in villages. From an early stage the temple and its administrators played a crucial role in the struggle to control political and economic activities in evolving towns.

Map II: Northern Iraq (Assyria), Syria and Eastern Turkey.

In Iraq at the outset of the *Ubaid* period (named after a site near Ur where it was first recognized), during the fifth millennium B.C., urban life was only a step away. Unfortunately this critical phase has not been so intensively researched on the ground as has the earlier period when farming communities emerged. However, on a theoretical level, hypotheses have multiplied to explain the precocious development of city-states in southern Iraq (ancient Sumer) in the fourth millennium B.C. There used to be a tendency to concentrate on single prime causes: on population pressure; on conflicts arising from wealth differentials in circumscribed agricultural land; on the need to organize centrally in order to run irrigation systems; and on the social and economic impact of long-distance trade in the quest for absent raw materials. Throughout these debates cause and effect were too easily confused, whilst other archaeological and anthropological evidence indicates that alone these factors do not necessarily have the required effect. Now the appearance of societies with a marked degree of status-ranking and complex literate administrative hierarchies, with a variety of functions, is interpreted increasingly in terms of multiple causes interacting in a particular environment.

Two factors may have been particularly important at the outset in Sumer. In a landscape where the value of land varied markedly with the availability of irrigation water for farming, the emergence of a socially stratified society was stimulated by inequalities in agriculture land-holding. At the same time the considerable insecurities of farming, the unpredictable rivers and floods, the dust storms and diseases, would have encouraged institutionalized social integration for self-preservation.

In the later fifth and earlier fourth millennium B.C. features characteristic of Ubaid culture spread down the shores of the Gulf and northwards along the Tigris and Euphrates. This suggests that the inhabitants of southern Iraq were already seeking to control access to the luxuries (gold and lapis lazuli) and raw materials and marine products vital to them. Already specialist industries manufacturing painted pottery, glazed materials (see p. 52), copper and gold, pointed the way to the fully-fledged craft traditions of the later Sumerian city-states in this region.

The critical phase in the emergence of these cities has long been associated archaeologically with the site of *Uruk* (Warka), where German excavations over many years have uncovered elaborate and impressive architecture in a phase known as "Uruk IV" in the mid-fourth millennium B.C. The town covered an area about 600% larger than any previous concentration of population, perhaps accommodating some 10,000 people. It has been estimated from surface surveys of ancient sites, recognized by distinctive pottery sherds on the surface, that in Sumer by about 3000 B.C. 50% of the population lived in villages, 21% in small towns and villages and 29% in larger towns, though none was so large as Uruk at its greatest.

19. **A clay tablet from Jamdat Nasr in Iraq, listing quantities of various commodities in archaic Sumerian, written in an early form of the cuneiform script; circles and half circles indicate numerals, c. 3200–3000 B.C. (Ht. 11 cm; 1926.564).**

Within the walled city of Uruk the temple complex was most conspicuous. Current work on the texts of Uruk IVa (see p. 46) may show whether there were already authorities ("kings") or wealthy private individuals other than those of the temple establishment. For the moment it is assumed that the temple administration largely controlled economic life by managing the farms upon which the whole community depended; collected, stored and distributed produce; "financed" full-time specialist craftsmen; and controlled the long-distance trade that brought in raw materials not available locally in exchange for agricultural produce and manufactured goods. It was in this context that writing developed, in its simplest pictorial form, to facilitate book-keeping (p. 46) hence the term "Proto-literate" often used to describe this period (pl. 19). The most distinctive of all artefacts from Iraq, the cylinder seal, also now emerged to supersede the stamp seal as a more effective marker of authority on the clay sealings placed on locks, packages and tablets (pl. 18).

Under temple patronage monumental building, large-scale sculpture in stone and metal, and fine craftwork in metal and organic materials flourished to an unprecedented degree. Through the quest for metals, stone and timber, agents from Iraq penetrated deep into the highlands. Recent excavations at such sites as Habuba Kabira on the line of the Euphrates in Syria, at Godin Tepe in central western Iran, and at Tepe Yahya deep into south central Iran, have revealed a network of surprisingly direct contacts. Intermediaries on the supply lines were cut out by establishing colonies along rivers and some sort of relationship with overland trading partners marked archaeologically by the widespread occurrence of pictographic tablets and certain distinctive types of pottery, notably simple coarse ware bowls with bevelled rims.

Links were established even with Egypt, where a state of a very different kind, centralized under an auto-

Map III: Southern Iraq (Sumer and Babylonia) and the Gulf (modern coastlines and river courses).

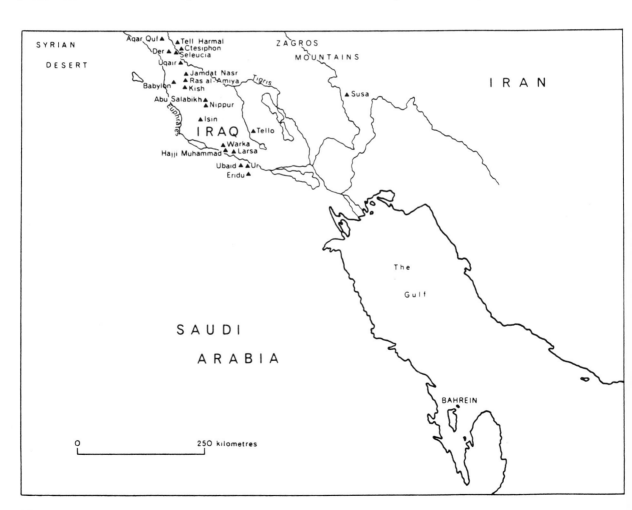

cratic monarchy combining secular and religious authority, was about to appear.★ Within the periphery, in many and various circumstances that still remain largely obscure, the seeds were planted for the emergence of town life in Turkey, Syro-Palestine and inner Iran in the third millennium.

Peoples of Historic Times, c. 3000–330 B.C.

In the earlier third millennium B.C. in modern studies of the ancient Near East "prehistory" (textless archaeology) begins to give way to "history" (text-aided archaeology). The convention is convenient, but misleading. Only in Egypt and Iraq at first, then later in parts of Syro-Palestine and Turkey, may written documents be used before the first millennium B.C. to reconstruct even the most minimal kind of history. Throughout, documents have little or nothing to say about the greatest number of people even in societies with scribes. The people in general are revealed, if at all, by the mute evidence of archaeology.

A second convention, again more convenient for purposes of synthesis than it is strictly accurate, takes modern Iraq (ancient Mesopotamia) as the focus of study. This area, and its interaction with its neighbours, is so fundamental to the history and cultural development of the ancient Near East that this oversimplification is excusable as the best way of presenting a sketch of the region between about 3000 B.C. and the campaigns of Alexander the Great (c. 330–323 B.C.), which led to a transformation of the region.

A: The Centre: Mesopotamia

Sumerians and Akkadians, c. 3000–2000 B.C.

The earliest settlers in southern Iraq for whom evidence at present exists, were established there in the sixth millennium B.C. occupying the fringes of marshes and lagoons. In the absence of hard evidence for any subsequent major change in population it is now assumed that *Sumerian*, the dominant language of the earliest texts two millennia later, was that of the earliest communities in the south. Later events and documents suggest that in northern Iraq it was the Semitic (*Akkadian*) language and Semitic and other settlers, from the neighbouring Syrian steppe and mountain hinterland, whose penetration characterized the later prehistoric period (cf. chart II).

From soon after 3000 B.C. there is increasing evidence for the history and organization of the Sumerian city-states of the south, most of them quite small. This, the earliest period for which king lists survive, is known as the *Early Dynastic Period*. There was a marked degree of economic interdependence. Intercity struggles, if frequent, were brief and localized. The earliest

★ See *Ancient Egypt* (Ashmolean Museum).

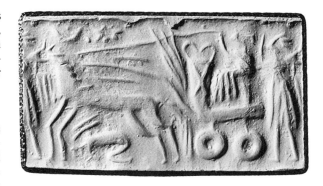

20. Modern plaster impression of a limestone cylinder seal from Kish in Iraq showing what may be a horse or one of its hybrids harnessed to a Sumerian heavy four-wheeled vehicle with solid wheels for a single occupant, c. 2500 B.C. (Ht. 32 mm; 1930.111).

ruler proved by a surviving inscription of his own time is Enmerbaragisi, c. 2700 B.C., last but one in the dynasty of Kish, which is that immediately after the flood in the "Sumerian King-List" (p. 11; pl. 9). During the period known to archaeologists as Early Dynastic III, c. 2600–2350 B.C., for the first time, economic and administrative texts and rare royal inscriptions, written in Sumerian, in the now developed cuneiform script, became plentiful enough to provide coherent, if meagre, information. Sumerian influence radiated far beyond their homeland. At Ebla deep into Syria, at Mari in the middle Euphrates, at Tell Chuera between the rivers Khabur and Balikh (tributaries of the Euphrates), at Assur on the Tigris, tablets, statuary and some small finds are virtually identical to those from Sumer.

Each Sumerian city was considered to belong to its main god to whom it had been assigned from creation and whose prestige rose and fell with the political fortunes of his main residence. The temple, his manor house, dominated the city, with its richly furnished mudbrick shrines, offices and workshops; the famous *ziggurats* or stepped towers of mudbrick may be a slightly later development. Its extensive fields and orchards, within and without the city, were rented out to share-croppers. Political power was wielded, in the name of the god, by a king (*lugal*: big man) or governor (*ensi*) who administered justice, directed military and external affairs, and acted as chief-priest. His residence and offices, with those of his court and family, came to rival in extent those of the temple. Apart from free citizens there was also a community of slaves with certain specific legal rights—prisoners of war, freemen enslaved for economic reasons or as punishments, children of the poor sold into bondage.

During Early Dynastic III the personal names of private individuals, and of a handful of gods and rulers,

21. Limestone statuette of a Sumerian man in an attitude of worship, originally placed in a temple as a perpetual token of respect to the gods; holes in the head for a headdress now lost; found by soldiers of the 14th Sikhs digging trenches at Istabalat, 20 km south of Samarra in Iraq, in 1917. (Ht. 20 cm; 1919.65).

the standardization of official documents, private letters and economic texts now written in Akkadian in the cuneiform script. It was a period of outstanding achievement in monumental sculpture and in the miniature reliefs cut on cylinder seals. Cylinder seals reflect as vividly as the great victory reliefs of the kings a new interest in portraying physical reality. The themes cut on the seals might be fantastic, but they were imagined and depicted much more concretely than before.

The Akkadian Empire, so much the creation of dynamic individual rulers, disintegrated rapidly in the face of internal dissensions and the pressure of such diverse foreign elements as the Elamites (p. 36), the Lullubi and Guti (mountain tribesmen from the Zagros), Hurrians (p. 35) from the north and Amorites (p. 26) about 2150 B.C. Some of the city-states of the south, notably Uruk and Lagash under its ruler Gudea, took advantage of the situation to revive their Sumerian traditions. In the event it was rulers of the *Third Dynasty of Ur* who briefly established a wide ranging dominion akin to that of Akkad. Two kings, Ur-Nammu and Shulgi, were largely responsible for the creation of this realm. Many thousands of Sumerian documents, primarily economic, attest a renaissance of the Sumerian language. The reign of Ur-Nammu was marked by extensive building activity, patronage of art and literature, and the earliest extant Sumerian "law code".

About 2000 B.C. this brief Empire collapsed, as had its predecessor, from the centre—weak royal authority encouraged devolution. City-states on the periphery of Sumer, at Assur, Mari and Susa, broke loose, and then overran the centres of power in the south, where for two or three centuries small city-states contended for independence in struggles polarised round the rival rulers of *Isin* and *Larsa*. The earlier part of the period, though of considerable economic and political uncertainty, saw a final flowering of Sumerian culture and the composition of such texts as the "king-list" (pl. 9) to stress the new rulers' legitimate claims to the timeless traditions of Sumerian kingship.

Amorites, Kassites and Chaldeans: Peoples of Babylonia, c. 2000–539 B.C.

When the Ur III Empire collapsed one of the chief instruments and beneficiaries of the change were the *Amorites*, semi-nomadic speakers of north-west Semitic dialects from the East Syrian steppe and desert. Their increasing presence in the population of southern Iraq at this time may be charted through their personal names in local texts. Most of the rulers of Larsa

indicate a progressive infiltration of Sumer by Semitic *Akkadians* from the north. But it was only through the energy of one man, Sargon, rising to power at Kish and then overthrowing the dominant Sumerian ruler of Uruk, that these people first came to rule over Mesopotamia, c. 2350 B.C. He established a new capital at Akkad (not far from the future site of Babylon) and by force of arms created a vast domain. Later traditions credited him with an Empire from the Upper Sea (the Mediterranean) to the Lower (Gulf).

Sargon paid due respect to the god Enlil at the Sumerian holy city of Nippur, but he appointed Akkadian governors and destroyed the walls of fortified Sumerian cities. The greatest of his successors, his grandson Naram-Sin, revived the Empire, but sacked Nippur and desecrated Enlil's shrine. The centralized organisation of the Akkadian Empire was reflected in

22. Sumerian gold and lapis lazuli jewellery from one of the famous "Death Pits" (PG 1237) in the Royal Cemetery at Ur in Iraq, c. 2500 B.C. (Pin = 16 cm long; 1930.219–22).

23. **Modern plaster impression from a shell cylinder seal of the Akkadian Period (c. 2350–2100 B.C.) in Iraq showing an ox drawing a plough fitted with a large seeder; bird swooping down to take scattered seeds. (Ht. 3.2 cm; 1969.346).**

24. **Modern plaster impression from a stone cylinder seal of the Akkadian Period (c. 2350–2100 B.C.) in Iraq showing worshippers before a seated god, with a whip; in the field: four long-haired sheep and two men with a large storage jar; inscribed "Kuli, king's officer(?), son of Kina". (Ht. 3.7 cm; 1967.1095).**

and Babylon bore Amorite names, and among the titles of Hammurabi of Babylon was "King of all the land of *Amurru*". It was he who, in a long reign c. 1792–1750 B.C., established Babylon as the capital of most of Iraq, through military campaigns and skilful diplomacy. Akkadian was now the dominant spoken language, used also for all written public and private business. Sumerian served on in the temples and their scribal schools as the language of learning. The most important single document of this period is Hammurabi's "law-code" inscribed on a stone obelisk now in the Louvre in Paris (see p. 45).

The reunification of Mesopotamia under Hammurabi barely survived him. Within the next one hundred and fifty years the extreme south was lost to the First Dynasty of the Sealand, rallying Sumerian traditions and loyalties. Pressures by Hurrians, Hittites and others accelerated the disintegration of the Babylonian state (p. 33). In circumstances of continuing obscurity, since there are no archaeological and very few historical sources, a people known as the *Kassites*, with distinctive language and social customs, then emerged as the ruling group. They may have gained this opportunity when, as mercenaries in Babylonia, recruited from tribes west of the middle Euphrates in Syria in the later seventeenth and early sixteenth century B.C., they were able to take advantage of a power vacuum.

By about 1400 B.C., when the documentary record reopens after a long 'Dark Age', the administrative capital had been moved to Dur Kurigalzu (Aqar Quf) near Baghdad. From the diplomatic archives of the contemporary Egyptian pharaohs found at Tell al-Amarna in Egypt (pl. 45), the Kassites emerge as a major power seeking through alliances and dynastic marriages to maintain their position. At home they had adopted the Akkadian language, creating a fresh literature in it; distinctly modified some aspects of art and architecture;

and established a semi-feudal social system with land grants recorded on small stone stelae (*kudurrus*) bearing a rich array of deity symbols to reinforce the curse formulas in the main text.

For over half a millennium from about 1200 B.C. Babylonia was overshadowed by Assyria. Local records and monumental art and architecture are very rare. Pressure by Aramaeans and others on her western frontiers left her weakened and royal authority much circumscribed (cf. p. 34). Only in the far south, safe from incursions, did Babylonian independence persist.

Here the *Chaldaeans* were to be found living along the lower courses of the Tigris and the Euphrates as vigorously independent tribes. Hence the biblical phrase 'Ur of the Chaldees' in *Genesis* 15:7. From the ninth century B.C. they were particularly effective opponents of intermittently growing Assyrian control, confining it largely to the main towns by guerrilla tactics. So effective was one of their rulers, Nabonassar (c. 747–734 B.C.), that later records regard his reign as a turning point, particularly in astronomical studies, subsequently especially associated with the term "Chaldaean". At this time the calendar was standardised, astronomical observations noted in systematic diaries with comments on the weather, river levels, etc., and major events recorded in a formal 'Babylonian Chronicle'.

When Assyrian power waned Nabopolassar (c. 625–605 B.C.), governor of the Sealand, usurped the throne and eventually in alliance with the Medes from Iran (p. 39) eliminated Assyrian power. His renowned son Nebuchadnezzar II (c. 604–562 B.C.) conquered the western provinces of the Assyrian Empire, sent the

25. **Baked clay head of a Babylonian woman with traces of the original painted decoration (formerly in the Bomford collection), c. 1800–1600 B.C. (Ht. 13 cm; 1976.74).**

Jews into captivity, and restored many Babylonian cities to their former splendour, for his dynasty were particularly interested in Babylonia's past. Numerous royal inscriptions, chronicles, private legal documents, and administrative texts, have made this, the Neo-Babylonian Period, one of the best-known in Babylonian history. Nabonidus (c. 555–539 B.C.) had a particular reverence for the moon-god Sin, reconsecrating the great temple at Harran for him, refurbishing his shrines at Ur and spending some ten years at Teima in Saudi Arabia, another cult-centre of this god. In 539 B.C. Babylon passed to the Persians under Cyrus (p. 40).

Assyrians: c. 2000–612 B.C.

The heartland of Assyria, named after its traditional centre at Assur, lay on the middle course of the river Tigris, expanding and retracting to north and south as opportunity offered. Restricted resources, regularly overextended by the creation of ephemeral empires, and recurrent instability in government circles were matched by a remarkable resilience. Although surviving sources may unduly emphasize the army's role, military power and prowess were clearly as crucial to Assyrian expansion as to her survival in a homeland without natural frontiers and particularly exposed to intruders from the steppe regions of Syria in the West.

It was no accident that from the fourth millennium, if not earlier, towns had grown up at Nineveh and perhaps also at Assur, since they were important as the focus of trade-routes linking Iran and Babylonia with Turkey. Business documents recovered from Kültepe in Turkey reveal the scope and organization of a trade in woollen textiles and tin from Assur, in gold and silver eastwards from Turkey, c. 1950–1750 B.C. (p. 32). The tin may ultimately have come from Afghanistan. It was not, however, until towards the end of the second millennium B.C., in the face of threats first by the Mitanni (p. 36) and then by the Aramaeans (p. 35) that the "land of Assur" emerged as a coherent political force. By then three primary trends in her subsequent dominance of the Near East had fully emerged.

Behind Assyria to north and east lay the mountain massif whence she derived vital raw materials, and horses for her armies. It was a region of chronic instability with marauding inhabitants restrained, and then only momentarily, by regular and exhausting military campaigns in the summer. Assyria's arch-enemy here, the state of *Urartu* (later historical Armenia) (p. 36), provided a bulwark which for centuries was placated or dominated as best served Assyria's ambitions. Ironi-

27. Clay tag from a bale of clothing, sent by the nobles of the court to King Shalmaneser III (c. 858–24 B.C.); stamped with the so-called "Royal Seal" showing the king in combat with a lion; from Nimrud (Mallowan's excavations). (Ht. 4.5 cm; 1954.739).

cally, it was the weakening of Urartu, with her own ambitions in the East, that opened the way to the Iranian-speaking Scythians and Medes (see p. 38), who were to contribute so much to Assyria's destruction in the later seventh century B.C.

To the west after the tenth century Assyria was the aggressor, first campaigning for loot and tribute, then establishing a territorial Empire to secure the land routes to rich ports on the Mediterranean coast, down to the borders of Egypt, also briefly subdued. Each succeeding major ruler from the earlier ninth to the seventh century B.C. had to contend with rebellion and defection in one or other part of his extended western realm, ever mindful as he campaigned deep into Syro-Palestine or Egypt that his eastern and southern flanks in Mesopotamia were dangerously exposed. And at court in Assyria there were always princes ready to take advantage of an absent king. Not only texts but also the reliefs carved in stone lining the lower inside walls of palaces at Khorsabad, Nimrud and Nineveh preserve in remarkable detail the armies and conquests of Assyria (pls. 1, 5, 11–12).

Assyria's relationship with her closest and oldest neighbour, Babylonia, was enduringly ambivalent. Babylonian deities entered Assyrian religion and the Babylonian literary tradition was adopted and assiduously cultivated. At Nineveh (whence in modern times much of it passed to the British Museum) Assurbanipal (c. 668–627 B.C.) had a library which may claim to be

26. Assyrian silver and gold finial, probably from the top of a helmet, from Nimrud in Iraq, c. 800–700 B.C. (Ht. 6.5 cm.; 1954.733).

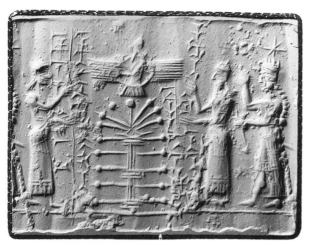

28. Modern plaster impression from a lapis lazuli cylinder seal showing the Assyrian king (in spiked headdress) Adadnirari III (c. 810–783 B.C.) with a goddess behind him; above the sacred tree hovers one of the major gods of Assyria in a disk; the figure to the left is probably the governor of Assur whose name appears in the inscription. (Ht. 48 mm; 1932.319).

the first ever assembled systematically, sometimes in the king's own words "for my own perusal". Gathered from all over Mesopotamia at the royal command it epitomizes the Assyro-Babylonian literary tradition at the end of its long history (p. 46).

With the death of Assurbanipal Assyria moved rapidly into eclipse. In 614–612 B.C. an alliance of Medes from Iran and Babylonians overran Assur, Nimrud and Nineveh; then in 605 B.C. the rump of the Assyrian army, allied with the Egyptians, was finally routed at Carchemish by Nebuchadnezzar and imperial supremacy passed briefly to Babylonia (p. 29).

B: The Western Periphery

Canaanites and Phoenicians; Philistines and Israelites

In between the older civilizations of Egypt and Mesopotamia urban life had developed in Syro-Palestine in the third millennium B.C. (Early Bronze Age). In Syria it seems to have followed the pattern earlier observed in Sumer to judge by finds at Mari and Ebla (Tell Mardikh), with their remarkable palace archives. The cities of Palestine were smaller and passed into temporary recession in the later third millennium, perhaps when commercial contacts with Egypt went into abeyance. Since *Canaanite* is the term used in the Old Testament to describe the major element in the population of Palestine at the entry of the Israelites in the twelfth century B.C., it is the best available generic term for the culture of Syro-Palestine in the Bronze Age, during which there is unlikely to have been any substantial change of population or linguistic

shift. Philologically Canaanite describes one branch of the North Semitic group of languages, including both Hebrew and Phoenician, the other branch being Aramaic (p. 51).

In the eighteenth and seventeenth centuries B.C. Palestine enjoyed a period of considerable material prosperity, though the archaeological record is intermittent and has to be supplemented by finds from richer sites in Syria like Alalakh (Tell Atchana) and Ugarit (Ras Shamra). A remarkable series of sealed tombs at Jericho contained a wide range of pottery and, most exceptionally of all, textiles, wooden furniture and utensils, basketry and food offerings. Bronze was increasingly used for weapons. Egyptian influence is conspicuous in various minor arts—notably furniture, alabaster vessels, and faience figurines (see p. 52),

Map IV: Major archaeological Sites in Canaan and the Kingdoms of Israel and Judah.

29. Baked clay model of a covered waggon with solid wheels of the type used in the steppe lands of northern Syria towards the end of the Early Bronze Age, c. 2400–2300 B.C.; said to be from Hammam near Carchemish (Jerablus). (Ht. 18.5 cm; 1913.183).

amulets and seals. In a manner not yet clearly determined northern Egypt was ruled towards the end of this period (Middle Bronze Age) by Asiatics (the *Hyksos*: "Princes of Foreign Countries") who drew much of their strength and culture from Palestine.

After the expulsion of the Hyksos from Egypt, c. 1550 B.C., Canaan became increasingly subject to Egyptian authority, politically and economically, though commerce linked her also to Cyprus and the Aegean. It was at this time that the Canaanites evolved their pre-eminent contribution to the civilized world: alphabetic writing. Whilst the Near East at large conducted its administrative, commercial and diplomatic affairs in the Akkadian language and the cuneiform script, in north and south Canaan, c. 1500–1200 B.C., unknown scribes devised the principle of an alphabet. Texts from Ugarit in a cuneiform alphabetic script and graffiti from Sinai in quasi-pictographic linear signs show diverse approaches to the same invention (p. 50; chart II).

The writers of the Old Testament largely ignored the cults of Canaan. Something of their character has been recovered through the discovery of texts at Ugarit giving vivid glimpses of the main deities and the more important festivals, rites and sacrifices at one important coastal town. They give life to the mute evidence of temple foundations, small metal statuettes of deities and other scattered pieces of cult furniture found on many sites in Syria and Palestine (pl. 34).

In the twelfth century B.C. the retreat of Egypt from Canaan exposed her to intruders. From the west came the *Philistines* (and other "Peoples of the Sea"). From the eastern and southern desert periphery the *Israelites* penetrated highland areas thinly populated by Canaanites. The kingdom of Saul and David emerged triumphant in the tenth century B.C. from the extended struggle between the Philistines and the Israelites. Canaan had by then passed into eclipse; but much of her culture survived in the north among the Phoenician cities, notably Tyre and Sidon, in what is now the Lebanon. The emerging states of Judah and Israel particularly, continued to be influenced by Phoenicia through close diplomatic and economic ties. Indeed Solomon's Temple in Jerusalem (I *Kings* 7) was architecturally, and in many of its fittings, a latter-day Canaanite structure through the use of Phoenician

**30. One faience and two gypsum cosmetic containers from
tomb G.37 at Jericho, c. 1800–1700 B.C. (Ht. 7.4 cm.; 8.4 cm.;
8.5 cm.; 1954.596–7, 1955.538).**

craftsmen, whose art was particularly characterized by
motifs derived originally from Egypt.

At home the *Phoenicians* were enterprising sailors
and merchant venturers who carried not only the commodities of the Levant west through the Mediterranean, but also the culture and skills of the Orient. If
the date and place of the adoption of an alphabetic
script by the Greeks remains controversial, none would
now question the ancient tradition that Phoenicia was
the ultimate source. A median date of 750 B.C. for its
full transmission seems likely, at a time when King
Pummay was ruling Tyre. As Pygmalion he made
more impact on Greek tradition than any other
Phoenician king. As writing involves writing materials,
it is no coincidence that the Greek word for book (*bub-
los* (papyrus)/*biblion* (book)) is thought to derive from
the name of the Phoenician city of Byblos.

Of all the peoples of the ancient Near East it is the
Israelites who need least introduction to the western
world, since their legacy through the Old Testament,
and a rich variety of other writings, survived throughout as a living tradition inspired by the unique religious
force of Judaism. Although this is no longer the isolated
phenomenon it once seemed to be, much remains to

be discovered about its origins on the periphery of
Canaan and the stages by which it became the only
dynamic culture to survive the impact of Hellenism
that changed so much else in the Near East towards the
end of the first millennium B.C.

C: The North and Northwestern Periphery

Hittites, Neo-Hittites and Aramaeans

The highland region of Turkey was the home of many
physically separated and independent groups of people
in contact both with the northern steppes and with the
heartlands of the Near East, which they supplied with
metals, stones and timber. Their material achievements
in the third millennium B.C. (Early Bronze Age) are
variously illustrated by famous finds from Troy
(Hissarlik) in the distant northwest and in "royal"
tombs at Alaça Hüyük in central Turkey. Sometime in
this millennium the *Hittites*, speaking an Indo-
European language later written in the cuneiform
script (chart II), established themselves on the central
plateau. Archives of cuneiform tablets in the Akkadian
language (chart II) from a colony established at Karum
Kanesh (Kültepe) in central Turkey, c. 2000 B.C.,
throw valuable light not only on long distance commerce at this time (see p. 29), but also on the illiterate
native population with whom the literate Assyrians
were trading (pls. 37, 40).

In about 1650 B.C. a ruler claiming to come from the city of Kushshar set up his capital at Hattusha, modern Boghazköy, and changed his name to Hattushili. Most modern knowledge of his people, the Hittites, until the fall of their Empire about 1200 B.C., is derived from objects and tablets found in the German excavations at Boghazköy.

Under the Hittite Old Kingdom (c. 1750–1550 B.C.) two kings, Hattushili and his successor Murshili, established military and diplomatic patterns that were to endure, although their own achievements were ephemeral. The Hittite kings sought to stabilize centres of power within a realm on the Turkish plateau that lacked secure natural frontiers, and was threatened on all sides. They were equally interested in control of profitable trade south-eastwards through Syria into Mesopotamia.

In a lightning campaign c. 1595 B.C. Murshili even succeeded in attacking Babylon. Throughout the period of the New Empire (c. 1400–1200 B.C.) the Hittite kings vied with the Egyptian pharaohs and the Mitannian rulers for control of the Euphrates trade route. When the Hittites were in the ascendant, a viceroy ruled from the fortress city of Carchemish (Djerablus). Little that was achieved by force of arms, diplomacy or international royal marriages endured without the energy of dynamic individual kings.

Hittite society in the second millennium B.C. is generally termed "feudal", though the implied medieval analogy is not precise. It was a complex, multi-lingual, ethnically mixed society, which had evolved slowly and did not attain the form best known from inscriptions until the New Empire. It incorporated administrative organs developed by the age-old village communities of peasant farmers in central

31. Jug painted in a distinctive style current in Syria in the early second millennium B.C. (Ht. 24.8 cm; 1967.1505).

32. Modern plaster impression from a haematite cylinder seal showing a Syrian ruler equipped as an archer, c. 1800–1700 B.C., in the newly introduced light-chariot with spoked wheels drawn by horses (compare pl. 20); escort of footmen. (21 × 10 mm; 1912.115).

33. Baked clay "stirrup jar" (restored)—a shape of Mycenaean Greek origin—in the distinctive painted style (red and black on a pale background) associated with the Philistines, c. 1150–1100 B.C., from Tell el-Farah (South) in Israel. (Ht. 12.5 cm; 1930.558).

Turkey, who underpinned the whole Hittite economic and social system. The king, who was viceroy on earth of the supreme storm god, owned the land, which he distributed as he willed, under ties of homage, to nobles, whose followers in turn owed them services. As in all feudal societies, they were bound to supply contingents of troops to the king when he required them.

The local religious cults, particularly, offer a microcosm of the diverse cultural heritage within the Hittite Empire. The chief gods of the state religion in the thirteenth century B.C. are spectacularly shown in processional reliefs in the rock-cut sanctuary of Yazilkaya, near the capital at Boghazköy, in central Turkey.

The Hittite Empire collapsed about 1200 B.C. from complex internal stresses and external threats, though its cultural legacy persisted into the so-called *Neo-Hittite* states of North Syria. Their rulers used the distinctive "Hieroglyphic Hittite Script" long known in Turkey, not to write Hittite itself but for a dialect of a language called Luwian (chart II). The major political and cultural centre at this time (c. 950–750 B.C.) was located at Carchemish. Here, as at other major Neo-Hittite sites, royal palaces and citadels were decorated with stone friezes and stelae that remain the best known monuments of these people. Pressure from the Aramaeans (see below), with their own city-states and cultural traditions, gradually superseded the last vestiges of Hittite culture in Syria.

Within Turkey, the centuries immediately after 1200 B.C. are barely illuminated either by texts or by archaeology. Only very slowly is information emerging about the *Phrygians*, who came to dominate the scene in the earlier first millennium B.C. from a capital at Gordium. Here excavations in huge burial mounds, one traditionally ascribed to the legendary king Midas, have revealed remarkable evidence for local craft achievements in painted pottery (see cover), bronze-work and inlaid wooden furniture in the eighth century B.C. At this time the Phrygians used a linear alphabet very close to that of the Greeks; but who adopted it from whom is an open question.

The *Aramaeans* were originally of nomadic or semi-nomadic origin with a homeland somewhere in the Syrian desert. When they first appear in Assyrian inscriptions in the later twelfth century B.C. they inhabit an area of Syria to the south-west of the Euphrates. They were a constant threat on Assyria's western frontier, seizing towns and disrupting communications. By the early first millennium B.C. there

34. Bronze statuette of an enthroned Canaanite ruler or god (the distinction is not certain) originally placed in a temple. (Ht. 9 cm; 1909.371).

were a series of Aramaean states in Syria above the great bend of the river Euphrates on both banks, intermittently southwards along the line of the river, and in inland Syria round Damascus. Tadmor, better known by its later name Palmyra, was also an Aramaean settlement.

By the later eighth century B.C. the Assyrians had broken Aramaean power in Syria; but they emerge as a dominant power in Babylonia a couple of centuries later. Many Aramaeans were deported and resettled in the Assyrian Empire, where they had an increasing impact on the practice of government and administration. Their most important cultural impact was through their language, Aramaic, written in a variant of the Phoenician alphabet. This was to become the diplomatic language of the Near East from the seventh century superseding Akkadian. It was largely written on wax tablets or perishable materials, rarely on clay tablets. Aramaeans are perhaps best known today through their appearances in the Bible, notably as formidable foes of David and the later kings of Israel, and for the famous words spoken on the cross by Christ in Aramaic: "*Elahi, Elahi* (given incorrectly as *Eloi*) *lama sabachthani?*—My God, My God, why have you deserted me?" (*Mark* 15:34).

Hurrians, Mitannians and Urartians

Among the most elusive, but most interesting, of the peoples of the ancient Near East are those who spoke the *Hurrian* language, perhaps of Caucasian origin, written in the cuneiform script (chart II). Having penetrated from the north in ever-increasing numbers from the mid-third millennium B.C. the Hurrians (Biblical *Horites*) may be recognized by their distinctive personal names in Mesopotamian texts. Texts in their own language were found in the palace at Mari on the Euphrates in Syria, in about 1800 B.C., when they were first referred to as a people. It may have been the Hurrians who particularly pioneered use of the light horse-drawn chariot with spoked wheels, new to the Near East, along with the training of horses to draw it and of archers skilled in taking advantage of a new mobile firing platform. So effective was this new weapon that scale-armour for men and horses was widely introduced to counteract it (pl. 32).

From about 1650 B.C. the Hurrians were regularly in conflict with the Hittites, particularly when they briefly formed a coherent state in north-east Syria

35. Restored fragment of carved ivory from a piece of wooden furniture, with sphinxes and a hieroglyphic inscription in the Egyptianizing style favoured by Phoenician craftsmen in the eight century B.C., from room SW 37 in Fort Shalmaneser of Nimrud, Iraq. The inscription is a garbled version of "Words spoken by Osiris" and would not have been placed in a royal cartouche (bracket), as here, by an Egyptian. (9 × 4 cm; 1960.1215).

36. Gold jewellery from Tell-Ajjul in Israel; the star and the "female"-pendants represent Canaanite fertility goddesses; sixteenth century B.C. (Gt. Ht. 8 cm; 1949.305–26).

known as *Mitanni*, ruled by an intrusive minority (c. 1500–1350 B.C.). The kings of Mitanni bore names associating them with Aryan intruders (cf. p. 39) and among their gods were such deities as Mitra, Varuna and Indra, later well known in northern India, as well as the Hurrian Teshup and Hepa. Their society was distinguished by a military aristocracy, which used chariots and received royal land grants in return for services. Until their capital *Washshukkanni* is located and excavated, their material culture will remain unknown, though certain types of painted pottery have been loosely associated with them. For a time the Mitannian state controlled much of Syria, including sites like Tell Atchana (Alalakh), Assyria and towns east of the Tigris, such as Nuzi, and maintained friendly diplomatic relations with Egypt to counter the strength of Assyria and the Hittites.

The Assyrians eventually superseded and absorbed the Mitannian kingdom, whilst the Hurrians became a submerged element when their language disappeared from records by 1200 B.C. In the first millennium B.C., round Lake Van in eastern Turkey, emerged a powerful state whose army was to rival that of Assyria and whose language, written in cuneiform, is in some way related to Hurrian. The *Urartians*, as these people are known, evolved a culture of their own with characteristic stone architecture, fine bronzework, and distinctive seals. Invaders from the north had crippled their state before it was absorbed by the Medes in the sixth century B.C.

D: The Eastern Periphery

Elamites and Iranians

The earliest historical records from Sumer indicate that the inhabitants of *Elam*, a long established state in south-west Iran, uniting the lowland plain of Susiana with its highland hinterland, were often in conflict with their neighbours. Although urban societies had developed about the same time in the fourth millennium at Uruk in Iraq and Susa in south-west Iran, each had drawn on strong local traditions that long served to distinguish them. Sumerian rulers in the middle of the third millennium penetrated deep into Iran, whilst the rulers of an Elamite city of unknown location, *Awan*, established a brief supremacy over Sumer. Excavations at Susa, whence most of the present archaeological information comes, have revealed corresponding fluctuations in the extent of Sumerian cultural influence. The Elamites still used their own pictographic script ("Proto-Elamite"), as yet only debatably deciphered, to write an unknown language that some have claimed

to be related to Dravidian, an ancient language of India, which may have been spoken over much of the Iranian plateau at his time. There is no real sign of Elamite political control east of Fars in central south Iran where the traditional capital of Elam, Anshan, was situated at Tepe Malyan near Persepolis. Yet there is evidence that trans-shipment centres in the third millennium B.C. (such as Shahr-i Sokhta and Tepe Hissar, far to the east, which handled lapis lazuli and other semi-precious stones, as well perhaps as tin, from Afghanistan) and production centres (such as Tepe Yahya in the Kerman region, which manufactured carved chlorite vessels) played some part in trading networks that linked Sumer through Elam with the fringes of Central Asia. Sumerian epics refer to the fabulous state of *Aratta*, deep in Iran, much as El Dorado ("the gilded one") featured in the imagination of the first explorers of South America. In one account, after much diplomatic activity, the king of Aratta sends gold, silver and lapis lazuli to the King of Uruk in exchange for grain. Mesopotamian demand for the

natural resources of the Iranian plateau may have stimulated the development there of urban societies with wealthy elites and specialist craftsmen.

The conquest of Elam by the rulers of Mesopotamia, c. 2300 B.C., had profound and enduring consequences for Elamite society. At first, inscriptions in the Akkadian language, using the cuneiform script, appear side by side with developed "Proto-Elamite" texts; but soon after no inscriptions seem to have been composed in the native language for hundreds of years. Akkadian, and the culture that came with it, seems largely to have taken over, though in language as in art certain traits reveal the persisting strength of local traditions. Relations with Babylonia continued to ebb and flow; the Elamites devastated Ur about 2000 B.C., and installed rulers in Larsa for sixty years, whilst Hammurabi of Babylon and some later Kassite kings subsequently exercised authority over Susa. Excavations at Haft Tepe, Susa and the great religious complex with a ziggurat and royal mausolea at Choga Zanbil in Khuzistan (in south-west Iran) have particularly indicated the individual strength of Elamite achievement in the fifteenth to thirteenth centuries B.C.

Within Iran, outside Khuzistan, the second millennium B.C. is still an archaeological and historical Dark

Map V: Iran.

37. Upper part of a baked clay envelope for a cuneiform tablet, with the seal of the Adad-Zululi archive from Karum Kanesh (Kültepe) in Turkey, c. 1900–1800 B.C., showing minor deities and worshippers before a seated goddess and the statue of a bull on an altar. (c. 50 mm square; 1968.65).

Age. A few linguistic indicators point to the migrations of peoples speaking Indo-European languages or dialects (p. 15; chart II) from north and east of the Caspian Sea into the vast region between the Ganges and the Euphrates. *Aryan*, with an approximate derived meaning of lord or noble, seems to have been the general ancient designation of these people; hence Iran: "land of the Aryans". In northern Iran the early Iranians may have been responsible for the remarkable pottery and the fine objects of precious and base metals excavated from a cemetery at Marlik, and retrieved by peasants illicitly from other sites in the region of Gilan known commercially as "Amlash", c. 1350–1000 B.C. (Pl. 10). In the early first millennium B.C. anonymous transhumant groups in the mountainous province of Luristan in Western Iran, drawing upon the age-old imagery of their mountain cults, created the remarkable ornaments, horse-equipment, "finials", and weapons in bronze commercially known today as the "Luristan Bronzes" (Pl. 43).

Medes and Persians, c. 700–330 B.C.

It is only when the Iranian-speaking peoples, of steppe origin, appear in Assyrian state records, the Persians in 844 B.C., the Medes in 836 B.C., that some picture of the main events in western Iran begins to emerge. At this time the Persians were established, in part at least, somewhere in Kurdistan; soon after 700 B.C. they

were far to the south-east in modern Fars (Persis), encroaching on Elam. The Medes, with their Scytho-Cimmerian confederates, were grouped round a capital at Ecbatana (Hamadan) on the eastern end of the main route through the Zagros Mountains from the Iranian plateau to the Mesopotamian plain. The many-columned halls of Persepolis have seventh century precursors at Godin Tepe and Nush-i Jan in Media; but little is known of the culture of either Medes or Persians at this stage.

38. Silver statuette (cut for use as scrap metal) of a god in Hittite style; bought by Sir Arthur Evans as from Nezero in Thessaly, Greece, c. 1450–1250 B.C. (Ht. 7.8 cm; 1896–1908 AE 410).

39. Hittite gold finger-ring for a man; winged deity standing on a sphinx with lion's head projecting from its chest; inscribed in "Hittite" hieroglyphic script "Great Prince". (46 × 14 mm; 1896–1908 0.6).

To this period some authorities date the great Iranian prophet Zarathustra (Greek Zoroaster). He lived in eastern Iran. His teachings have survived in some of his hymns (the *Gathas*), which, though revealing a knowledge of the traditional mythology of the Aryans, give a profoundly philosophical interpretation of the Universe. He proclaimed a single supreme God, creator of all things, beyond the reach of evil forces. The world, he taught, was divided between two opposite poles of Good and Evil, Truth and Lie, offered as free choices to all humanity. The supreme symbol of Truth is fire and fire-altars are consequently the primary cult symbol of Zoroastrianism (pl. 45).

Iran fully entered world history under the Persian king Cyrus 'the Great' (c. 559–530 B.C.), who welded the Medes and the Persians into a coherent state and exploited to the full the fine army he had inherited, to conquer much of Western Asia, beginning with the states of Assyria and Babylon. Upon the basis he established his immediate successors, outstandingly Darius I (c. 522–486 B.C.), created the greatest of all Near Eastern Empires, extending from the Aegean to the Indus, from Arabia to the Caucasus. Within Iran their great monuments survive in ruined state at Pasargadae, the coronation city and burial place of its founder Cyrus I, and at Persepolis, creation of Darius I, whither the monarchs came in life on fixed occasions to celebrate the achievements of their ancestors through religious ceremonies and diplomatic receptions and in death to be buried. Here, and in palaces at Babylon and Susa, craftsmen created a court style, in glazed brick and sculptured friezes, entirely distinctive of the new imperial overlords, though using the traditional iconography of the superseded Assyrian and Babylonian kings.

Throughout the Empire the presence of rich patrons attached to the courts of the local governors (satraps) stimulated local craftsmen to adjust their traditional skills and styles to the new taste in gold and silver plate, jewellery, fine cut-glass and pottery vessels, particularly to the Iranian love of animal ornament and colour contrasts. Yet much went on in traditional ways in the wealthy provinces of Egypt, Phoenicia and Babylonia, and the ancient kingdoms of Lydia and Phrygia in Turkey. The Persian Empire did little to change the basic character of life for most people in the Near East. It was the Hellenic culture which emanated from Greek colonies and merchants established in the region after Alexander the Great's conquests in 330–320 B.C. that profoundly modified it.

E: The Southern Periphery

The Arabs

The peoples of the Arabian Peninsula before the advent of Islam in the seventh century A.D. still tend to be known more widely through their Biblical names (Dedanites; Ishmaelites; Midianites; Sabaeans, etc.) than by the generic term "Arabs", which means simply "nomads". Throughout history there has been a difference and a degree of antipathy between the Arabs of the North and of the South within the Peninsula. The latter developed a particularly distinctive early civilization, which archaeology has increasingly elucidated in recent decades.

The inhabitants of the southwest in the first millennium B.C. were great builders and skilful creators of agricultural systems based on terracing and the careful storage and distribution of scarce water. The overland spice trade brought them wealth and regular contacts with their neighbours to the north in southern Palestine and Jordan. In the Old Testament references to *Seba* mean the Sabaeans of modern Yemen, whereas *Sheba*, whence came the famous Queen, may have been further to the north.

The peoples of the southwest learnt an alphabet from the north and adapted it to their own purposes in writing a number of local dialects. Thousands of inscriptions have survived. Though few are of any great length, they contain relatively abundant information on political, social and religious life. Details of chronology, however, remain subjects for lively debate. Alabaster funerary statuettes (pl. 46) and inscribed stelae, many of them routine and uninspired,

40. Jug of the type associated with the Assyrian trading colony at Karum Kanesh (Kültepe) in central Turkey in the early second millennium B.C. (Ht. 43 cm; 1921.1073).

41

41. Faience container from Iran; c. 700 B.C. (Ht. 11.2 cm.; 1976.75).

42. Glazed terracotta jar said to be from Iran; c. 1300 B.C. (?) (Ht. 9.9 cm.; 1971.981).

and small incense burners, are the commonest artefacts reported from the area.

When they appear on Assyrian palace sculptures the Arabs of the north, of whom relatively little is yet known, are shown fighting from camels and with tents much like those of the modern Bedouin. The importance of the oasis city of Teima, where the Babylonian king Nabonidus spent a long period in the earlier sixth century B.C. (p. 29), is historically evident but still archaeologically obscure.

The *Nabataeans* appear to have been the only northern Arabs to have created a civilization comparable to that in the southwest of the Peninsula. They had established themselves in ancient Edom, with a centre at Petra, after the end of the Achaemenid Persian Empire and flourished particularly from the first century B.C. to the second century A.D. Petra prospered on the camel caravan trade which passed through to Syria and Palestine bringing goods from southern Arabia, the horn of Africa, India and beyond.

Recent surveys have shown Nabataean mastery in creating an agricultural economy, by skilful conservation of scanty water supplies, in areas apparently bleak and inhospitable. Cities, villages and forts in the Negev of modern Israel and in Transjordan demonstrate that their architectural genius was no less impressive. One of their most distinctive achievements was a very thin pottery, generally bowls, painted with stylized floral and leaf patterns. Qumran, source of the "Dead Sea Scrolls" (p. 51), fell within the area of Nabataean influence and the first Nabataean papyri were found in caves there.

Archaeological research has also progressed dramatically in recent years in Eastern Arabia with marked concentration on the Island of Bahrein, and the adjacent parts of Arabia, and in Oman at the entrance to the Gulf. The copper resources of Oman and the role of

Bahrein as a staging post for goods travelling to Mesopotamia from Iran and the Indian subcontinent, from at least the third millennium B.C., have been the primary themes in this research. The role of this intercultural contact in stimulating the development of distinctive cultures in the Gulf area is still under investigation; but already the Bronze and Iron Age settlements of the region are increasingly seen as an important independent phenomenon in the vast panorama now offered by the ancient Near East.

3. Aspects of Daily Life

I: The Service of the Gods

Religion and its ritual permeated life in most societies in a way difficult to imagine in a modern western state. Law and government, art and craft, and the entire range of written record and intellectual life in complex urban communities, were deeply rooted in religious observance and temple service. In daily life events and unusual happenings were traced back to the agency of the deities, who were manifold, not to natural or historical causes. Even in the religion of Israel, exceptional in so many ways in its developed form, the powerful legacy of the polytheistic Canaanite religion at first isolated it less than might now seem to be the case.

Generally religious practice had two very distinct aspects, the one more fully understood than the other. The state or official religion was an exclusive cult, the

43. Bronze decorative harness ring for a horse from Luristan in western Iran, c. 900–700 B.C. (8.6 × 8.4 cm; 1965.196).

present in it, whether it was a statue of the most precious materials and finest craftsmanship or a cheap replica. The gods were believed to move with their images when carried off by victors in war, thus expressing their anger. Images or religious symbols were the focal points for sacrificial activities in temples and in open-air ceremonies. The main deity of a settlement lived in a temple, regarded as his "house", in a way that paralleled in key respects the life of a chief or a king at court. In Mesopotamia, for instance, he would be clothed and served meals in a manner appropriate to a monarch.

In many societies the arts of the diviner held a crucial role as the means through which men and gods communicated. They sought to ascertain the will of the gods who, it was assumed, in their turn were open to such contact and to appropriate rites to avert their wrath or displeasure. Techniques of divination varied widely and are best known from Assyro-Babylonian texts. They included the interpretation of significant traits in animals' entrails; in the action of smoke in air or oil in water; in the behaviour of birds and animals, celestial and other natural phenomena; and in dreams. The role of prophets in communication between gods and men is more evident in Syro-Palestine than in ancient Iraq. Indeed the Hebrew prophets emphasize the difference by mocking Babylonian divination, elsewhere regarded as a powerful intellectual achievement. "Chaldaean" long served in English as a word for soothsayer or seer (cf. p. 26).

Only in very rare cases, in marked contrast to Egypt, did the concept of the king as a god take root. Generally he was seen as the representative on earth of the gods, particularly of the chief deity in any pantheon. In this role the king had duties both to his masters, the gods, and to his subjects, as warleader and the fountainhead of justice and guarantor of social order.

The special relationship of ruler and gods was conspicuously marked by his activity as builder and restorer of their "houses": the city temples, and by his role as high-priest, especially in regular rituals designed to symbolize the intimacy of the relationship. Good fortune in affairs of state was attributed to divine favour, ill-fortune to divine displeasure. The ruler's duty was to know the mind of the gods (through diviners) and to humour them. Proper performance of the rituals intimately linked rulers and deities and were regarded as essential to prosperity in peace, success in war.

The king was the lawgiver, as deputy for the god of justice, and guarantor of its right administration. This was more of a social than a religious obligation, originating in the role of the tribal chief expected to be accessible and impartial in his dispensation of justice to all. He was required to concern himself as much with debt collection and fair regulation of prices as with

preserve of the priests in temple communities which served the gods in private. The complex theology and mythology that texts preserve of this side of religious life can have meant little to the illiterate population at large. Their religious beliefs have to be gleaned from mute archaeological evidence, primarily statuettes and plaques, amulets and charms. It was only through occasional public festivals in the towns that the people were drawn into temple worship and then only as spectators in special performances. It was not the "Great Gods" (pls. 24, 28) so much as the deities and demons who might be expected to relieve the dangers and burdens of daily life who appealed most widely.

In the imagination of men the world of the gods was conceived exactly as that of a king (compare pl. 34), his extended family and his aristocracy. The members of the other world were believed to behave very much as did their human counterparts. When represented in art they appear in human form, variously distinguished, or are represented by their familiar animals and by inanimate symbols. Major deities were generally few in number. Minor deities and demons, benevolent and evil, were numerous. Gods represented the celestial bodies, the forces of nature and the skills of hand and intellect. Goddesses embodied fertility and maternity, both passively and actively, sometimes combining the roles of divine consort and warrior-goddess.

In the cult of temples, as in household shrines, the image was central since the deity was considered to be family law and petty crime. Hammurabi of Babylon's famous "Law Code", inscribed on a basalt stela, standing 2.25 metres high, in 49 vertical columns, in the eighteenth century B.C., is not a code in the strict sense, rather a record addressed to the gods of his deeds as a just king: "These are the laws of justice which H. the able king has established . . . That the strong may not oppress the weak, to give justice to the orphan and the widow . . ."

It is deities and kings who feature time and time again in the Court Art of the ancient Near East wherever it survives. In acts of war, of hunting, or of worship the king recurrently acknowledges his debts to the gods in reporting his prowess and successes in pictures. In Popular Art it is nude female figurines and various popular demons or symbols and motifs designed to avert evil that recur time and time again (pl. 42), varying only to suit the tastes of diverse peoples and succeeding generations. Symbols of fertility are the one most constant link between the imagery of official and of popular religion; seeking to ensure on the one hand the fertility of the land upon which all life depended, on the other of the human mother who sustained the extended family that formed the basis of every social unit.

II: Languages and Literature (see chart II)

For purposes of comparative study scholars classify languages into families united by their conformity to certain general "laws" of word structure and phonetics. Two such linguistic families predominated in the ancient Near East: the *Semitic*, to which many of the modern languages of the area also belong, and the *Indo-European*, the family which includes English. But there are a number of very important dead languages now known in the Near East that elude these academic categories and remain unclassified. They include, notably, the Sumerian language, the first ever written down (cf. p. 22), the related Hurrian and Urartian languages (cf. p. 36), and Elamite.

44. Boot-shaped vase from northwest Iran, c. 1000 B.C. (Ht. 11 cm.; 1965.755).

45. Modern plaster impression of a cylinder seal, bought in Egypt, showing priests in Persian costume officiating at a fire-altar in which a boar appears to be suspended; Fifth to fourth centuries B.C. (3.4 × 1.3 cm; 1892.1416).

Nothing is certainly known of the languages spoken in the Near East before the appearance of written evidence. There has been much speculation about the early distribution of these linguistic families and their precursors, since some place-names have been taken to indicate a pre-Semitic linguistic substratum in Syro-Palestine and a pre-Sumerian one in southern Iraq. At present the Semitic and unaffiliated languages are generally thought to have evolved south of the Caucasian mountains. The ultimate source of the Indo-European tongues remains more controversial. Whether the earliest recorded, like Hittite, came originally from the steppe region of south Russia, as did the later Iranian language (cf. p. 39), or evolved within the Near East in prehistory, is disputed.

The Mesopotamian Tradition

Since the cuneiform script, and the languages it expressed, finally disappeared from use in the first century A.D., when both political and cultural circumstances were hostile to the tradition that had created and used it, a fundamental role has been played in modern times by scholars who at critical stages pioneered decipherment.

In the first decade of the nineteenth century the way was opened by the German scholar Grotefend, who worked with trilingual royal inscriptions of the Achaemenid Persian Period from Iran written in the Babylonian (Akkadian), Elamite and Old Persian languages in various cuneiform scripts. As Old Persian has a sister language, then known as Zand, already to some considerable extent understood, it was the ultimate key to decipherment of Akkadian. It was still to be over fifty years before, in 1857, the French scholar Oppert

was able to give the first translation of an Akkadian text without the help of an Old Persian version.

In the meanwhile outstanding contributions to the decipherment of Old Persian and Akkadian had been made by the English scholar Rawlinson. Hincks, an Irishman, was the first to recognize as early as 1850 that the cuneiform script had been invented by a non-Semitic people and only later adopted to write the Semitic language Akkadian. In 1869 Oppert identified the inventors as the Sumerians and by 1873 Lenormant had outlined the primary characteristics of their language. The following century has seen great advances in the study both of Sumerian and Akkadian, and of those other ancient languages, now dead, once written in cuneiform, such as Hurrian and Urartian (see p. 36) and the Indo-European language Hittite (p. 32).

A pictorial script (pl. 1) first emerges in the archaeological record about the middle of the fourth millennium B.C., predominantly at Uruk in south Mesopotamia at a time when it was the major town in the region. In time the pictographs developed into the stylized combinations of wedges known as *cuneiform* (pl. 9). From the outset numbers had been written with strokes to indicate units and a circular impression, sixes or tens (compare pl. 19). As single cuneiform signs came to have many different "pronunciations" or readings the system was complex, requiring special training to use and thus confined to a prestigious class of scribes.

For modern scholars the purely technical difficulties of transliteration and translation are accentuated by the arbitrary selection of texts that has survived. They concentrate in certain places and certain periods and come predominantly from public buildings. Attempts by modern scholarship to penetrate the meaning and function of archives is complicated by the fact that here, as in every bureaucracy, much is taken for granted and not written down, whilst concepts are described in terms remote from modern experience.

Yet still it is in these documents that we come closest to the rich variety of life in ancient Mesopotamia to a degree that even the surviving records of Egypt, Greece or Rome rarely permit. The people themselves emerge most vividly in their *letters*, ranging from formal royal correspondence to the petty concerns of private individuals. The more formal side of their daily life is to be glimpsed in all kinds of legal documents regulating family life as much as the place of the individual within the wider social and economic system. Tantalisingly incomplete glimpses of religious life and thought may be gleaned from fragmentary *prayers, hymns and incantations, ritual instructions* and *god-lists.*

46. Alabaster statuette of a man, inscribed "Dhara'karib (of the clan) Madrarum" from Nugub, near Beihan, in South Yemen; first to second century A.D. (?). (Ht. 27.5 cm; 1954.752).

In marked contrast, and usually more meaningful to the modern view are the more *scientfic texts*: recipes for alloying metals or for making glazes and glazed materials; mathematical problems and solutions; astronomical observations, medical lore typical of folk medicine everywhere; and topographical descriptions of cities like Babylon. However, the introduction of mathematics into astronomy, a crucial step, did not take place until after the middle of the first millennium B.C.

Of all documents two groups, the omen (or divination) and the "lexical" texts, are particularly distinctive of this culture. "*Omen texts*" list the effects to be expected by realms or individuals from a whole series of (to us) sometimes bizarre symptoms: eclipses or the positions of the stars (astrology); dreams and unusual daily events, physical abnormalities in animals and men; and the markings of liver and lungs in sacrificial animals. It is in the "*lexical texts*", however, that the Sumerians and Babylonians are revealed as inveterate cataloguers. Fundamental to the education of a scribe were systematic lists of all natural phenomena and man-made objects, originally compiled in Sumerian from the earliest phase of writing (Uruk IV), with Akkadian translations added later; a remarkable bonus for modern scholarship. So far as we know this accumulation of information in long lexical lists was an end in itself, not the basis for generalizations.

In any written traditions the modern reader would seek particularly for *literary* and *historical texts*; both exist in the Mesopotamian legacy, but in distinctive forms. Broadly speaking the "classic" works of literature follow a pattern of development: the original is in Sumerian with the first Akkadian version written down in the first half of the second millennium B.C. Then copying, compiling and editing went on generation after generation, with new texts emerging as Akkadian gradually ousted Sumerian. The last great Assyrian king Assurbanipal (c. 668–627 B.C.) formed in his palace at Nineveh an enormous library of tablets which was discovered in the nineteenth century and is now largely in the British Museum. This remains our primary guide to the Mesopotamian literary tradition, since so many of the standard texts studied and transmitted through the training and education of scribes were represented in it.

The major surviving *epics* touch on matters of enduring and universal human relevance seeking, often in remarkably evocative poetry, to explain the primary dilemmas of human life and the mysteries of the natural and supernatural world. Gods and goddesses, conceived in human form with human vices and virtues, are presented dispassionately, sometimes in the company of legendary kings of Sumer, such as Enmekir and

Gilgamesh of Uruk. The latter's unsuccessful quest for immortality is a primary theme in the famous epic now named after him. In one episode (that has an independent origin), Utnapishtim, the Babylonian Noah, relates the famous story of the Flood that electrified Victorian England with its echoes of *Genesis* when first translated. Another shorter epic, the creation story of *Enuma elish* ("when on high") relates the rivalries and contests of gods and demi-gods through which the universe and mankind were created, extolling particularly Marduk, the tutelary god of Babylon. It was recited at the New Year's festival in the city.

Texts from Mesopotamia referring to the past or to contemporary events focused exclusively on rulers and their families, not on the people as a whole. Royal inscriptions in Sumer and Babylonia primarily described building activities and rarely referred to military activity, whilst in Assyria great emphasis was placed on both (pl. 1). *Historical writing*, as it would be most generally understood today, was not a feature of this tradition, though the seeds of it may be detected in the "Chronicles" of the Neo-Babylonian period from the seventh into the sixth centuries B.C.

More typical are the "King-Lists" of Sumer, Babylonia and Assyria which take their place among the useful lists of all kinds characteristic of Mesopotamian writings. The Sumerian King-List (pl. 9) was written down about 1800 B.C. to tell how kingship came down from heaven first to the city of Eridu in southern Iraq. Eight or nine rulers who ruled in five cities were then named and credited with reigns of epic length. A flood that swept over the earth ended this period after which kingship again descended, this time on Kish. Groups of kings over individual cities were then listed as if they had ruled over Sumer consecutively, whereas many had been contemporaries. The compiler wished to present a specific conception of the past suited to a particular political purpose rather than an accurate chronological list in the modern sense.

Much of this literature circulated in the closed world of the scribes, who alone could read and write it; much of it was private communication between kings and their gods buried in foundation deposits. We do not know to what extent a wider audience was acquainted with literary texts through public readings or mimed representations. That there was an orally transmitted folklore is reflected in written collections of *proverbs and riddles*. It may be that our impression of Mesopotamia's culture has been unduly distorted by what has survived in the intellectual legacy preserved in the libraries of temples and palaces.

The Syro-Palestinian tradition

Cuneiform tablets from Byblos in the Lebanon c. 2100 B.C. and archives discovered during the 1970s at ancient Ebla (Tell Mardikh) in a palace of the mid-

47. Pottery vessel in the shape of a man pouring a libation, Luristan, Iran, c. 800 (Ht. 24 cm.; 1971.982).

48. Translucent light red jasper seal, with a modern plaster impression of the design; inscribed in Hebrew script for a lady called Hannah, with a sphinx derived from Phoenician art, which used many motifs previously fashionable in Egypt and Canaan. Found on the surface at Tell ed-Duweir (Lachish) in the early 1940s. (26 × 19 mm; Gibson Loan).

third millennium B.C. indicate that there was a much wider spread of the cuneiform script than used to be thought probable at such an early date. They indicate that cuneiform had been current in the region where the alphabet was later to emerge, raising the possibility that it might have influenced this remarkable invention. It is, however, still generally argued that the alphabet is "consonantal", like ancient Egyptian, not "syllabic" like Akkadian, and that it was through contacts with literate Egyptians that Canaanites in the Middle Bronze Age conceived the alphabet (cf. p. 30) not through contacts with literate peoples in Syria or Iraq.

Exactly where and when this happened is still uncertain. In 1905 Petrie's excavations at Serabit el-Khadim in Sinai revealed several short inscriptions in an unknown pictographic script carved by Semites working in the local turquoise mines for Egyptians. Many more have been reported from Sinai since then. These "Proto-Sinaitic" inscriptions are now dated about 1500 B.C. They have not yet been fully deciphered, but quite a number of the pictographs, limited to 27 letters in all, have been identified as the original forms of the later Phoenician letters that travelled to Greece in the earlier first millennium B.C. to constitute the alphabet we use. However, from Gezer, Lachish and

Shechem in Palestine have come short pictographic inscriptions ("Proto-Canaanite") that may be a century or two older, so complicating the picture. Be that as it may, this was a West Semitic or Canaanite invention. The stance of letters depended on the direction of writing which was still flexible. Each sign represented a consonant plus a vowel; an abstraction and simplification not achieved earlier and essentially an alphabetic system of writing.

Now for the first time, in theory at least, literacy was put within the range of many more people and it has been argued that by the Iron Age in Palestine there was a greater degree of general literacy than in those countries where the much more complex cuneiform writing system endured. However, until modern times, it is very unlikely that more than a tiny minority in any country could read or write in the strict sense. The ability to write one's own name, or to recognize it when cut on a seal as became common in the time of the Divided Monarchy in Israel or Judah, is not a mark of literacy in any real sense (pl. 48).

So far the major witness to the scribal literary tradition of Canaan has been provided by archives of clay tablets from Ras Shamra, ancient Ugarit, in Syria, dating to the fourteenth and thirteenth centuries B.C. These include tablets written in Akkadian in the syllabic cuneiform script, traditional in Mesopotamia, and a new version, with thirty signs, in which the wedge-shaped script is adapted to the alphabetic principle to write administrative documents, letters and literary works in the local language known today as "Ugaritic" (Chart II).

49. Fragment of a mosaic glass goblet and a faience cosmetic pot from Tell Rimah, Iraq, c. 1300 B.C. (Ht. 4.5 cm.; 1966.182; Ht. 7 cm.; 1966.162).

The cults of the Canaanites were heavily abused by the writers of the Old Testament. It is only now that we may begin, through the Ugaritic texts, to appreciate their fundamental importance for a full understanding of the earliest religious ideas and cult practices of the Israelites. The vocabulary, literary forms and style of the mythology and poetry recorded in the Ugaritic texts has elucidated the earliest sections of the Old Testament, such as the *Song of Deborah*.

By at least the eleventh century B.C. the main-line alphabetic scripts of the first millennium B.C., the Aramaic, the Hebrew and the Phoenician, may be seen emerging from the complex earlier tradition of Canaanite scripts, though significant archaeological finds from the transitional period are rare and their firm dating often difficult. Surviving texts are short or very fragmentary; the education and role of scribes in this society has still largely to be reconstructed from biblical sources.

As the vast majority of "Early Hebrew" (or palaeo-Hebrew) documents were probably written on papyrus or leather much has perished and the witness of archaeology is inevitably very circumscribed. The major extra-biblical inscriptions relevant to Israel and Judah all come from Mesopotamia.

Two main styles may be defined in the development of the Hebrew script before the later first millennium B.C., both revealed by archaeology in recent times and each corresponding more or less to well-defined groups of artefacts. First, monumental or lapidary script is found on such rare historical inscriptions as that in the Siloam Tunnel at Jerusalem, cut by King

Hezekiah's masons, c. 700 B.C., as well as on the much more numerous baked clay stamped jar handles, inscribed stone weights and seals of the eighth and seventh centuries B.C. (pl. 48).

A cursive or more practical every day script was used for writing in ink on ostraca (pieces of stone, pot or bone) as in famous groups from Samaria of the eighth century B.C., and from Arad and Lachish of the early sixth century B.C. They tell us something of administrative procedures; but in no way yet match the wealth of contemporary evidence preserved on tablets in Mesopotamia. A very rare survivor is a fragmentary letter on papyrus, dated by palaeographic criteria to the eighth century B.C., found in the caves of the Wadi Murabbaat, west of the Dead Sea.

The "Square Hebrew" script, ancestor of the modern Hebrew alphabet, is not a direct descendant of the palaeo-Hebrew script, but of the Aramaic script which was used internationally in the period of the Persian Empire, c. 550–320 B.C. It became standardised just before the Christian era and many famous papyri found since 1947 in caves along the western shores of the Dead Sea are inscribed in it.

All the original versions of the individual writings that go to make up the Old Testament have perished or so far eluded excavators. Prior to 1947 the earliest Hebrew manuscript of any part of the Old Testament went back no earlier than the early eleventh century

A.D., with some fragments reaching back a few centuries earlier. The discovery of the "Dead Sea Scrolls" radically changed this. They included fragments of all biblical writings except *Esther*, including one complete and one partial copy of *Isaiah*. Some are now dated to the third, possibly to the fourth, century B.C., and the complete *Isaiah* scroll may date about 150 B.C. With these biblical texts were many sectarian works generally associated by scholars with a community at Qumran, close to the Dead Sea, commonly identified as Essenes, dispersed about 70 A.D. as Rome moved to suppress the First Jewish Revolt.

Other Traditions

In a survey as brief as this there is always the danger that major original contributions to the literature of the ancient Near East will be overlooked, since they fall outside the range of the Old Testament World. This applies particularly to the Hittite and Hurrian scribal traditions in which legends and tales, as well as royal annals and related documents, have a distinctive character of their own. Then again, as has already been briefly noted (p. 39), the Iranian-speaking peoples enjoyed their own written legacy of sacred texts and epics generally known today only from much later versions.

III: The Creativity of Craftsmen

Although techniques generally spread further and more easily than languages and religious concepts, modern knowledge of their passage is often more elusive, since it depends wholly on the survival of artefacts. Organic materials decay and disappear; metal is constantly re-cycled; only stone and baked clay endure, albeit often damaged. At all times, not least in the nomadic and semi-nomadic societies of this region, the working of wood, of leather, of reeds, and of textiles were major crafts. Isolated glimpses of what has gone for ever include: wood-work from tombs at Jericho about 1800–1600 B.C.; scraps of textiles or basketry from various sites; unique burnt wooden carvings from Ebla c. 2400 B.C.; and richly embroidered robes depicted on polychrome glazed-bricks from Susa, c. 500 B.C. Even the most detailed written lists of royal gifts or commodities issued to craftsmen for specific tasks are no substitute for what has been irretrievably lost. It has always to be remembered that the craft inventory as it now appears in museum displays is a highly impoverished one.

The working of *stones* first through flaking, then also through grinding and polishing, was established in the Near East at an early date; by the time of the first settled farming communities in Western Asia the texture and colour of various stones were also exploited as appropriate for tools or containers, ornaments or seals.

Obsidian from Turkey, lapis lazuli from Afghanistan, and turquoise from Sinai and Iran, widely traded from an early date, testify to a taste for exotics. These skills endured, though stone vessels grow rarer after about 2000 B.C.

The *use of fire*, whether in ovens, in kilns or in furnaces and beneath crucibles, was ingeniously manipulated in the early farming communities to transform a variety of materials: lime for plaster and vessels; clay and mineral pigments for painted pottery; lead and copper (later gold and silver) for trinkets and small tools. As a consequence it was soon appreciated that heating carved steatite increased its hardness sixfold and that painting it with blue and green mineral pigments, and then firing it, gave it a vitreous coloured glaze of high and durable gloss. Dull coloured stones could thus be made to imitate expensive semi-precious ones.

By the fourth millennium B.C. craftsmen were already blending such chemicals as lime, soda and silicates (sand of quartzite) in combination with mineral colourants to produce glass-like compositions (*frit and faience*). Free-modelled or moulded they serve as the basis for an extensive manufacture of beads and amulets, with a much more restricted production of small statuary and vessels (pl. 49).

The emergence of *true glass* moulded like faience or core-formed for the same range of artefacts, in the middle of the second millennium B.C., permitted opaque coloured semi-precious stones (both monochrome and polychrome), to be more effectively imitated (pl. 49). It was not until the eighth and seventh centuries B.C. that an ability to manufacture clear glass, in imitation of the then popular rock crystal, is first evident. From the sixteenth century B.C. baked clay pottery and bricks had also been decorated with alkaline glazes in some areas, bringing much needed colour to the craft of builder and potter. But it was not until about 75–50 B.C., perhaps somewhere in Phoenicia or Syria, that unknown craftsmen perfected the art of glass-blowing.

Although *pottery* has been recognized from the outset as the ABC of archaeology, it is only very recently that studies of the technical expertise involved in the selection and blending of raw materials, in the use of construction techniques, in decoration and in firing, begin to permit a proper description of the ubiquitous pottery industries of the ancient Near East. With rare exceptions, like the burnished pottery of Northwest Iran ("Amlash") (pl. 10) in the Iron Age or the painted wares of the same period in Phrygia in Turkey (cf. cover picture) the most memorable pottery of the Near East in antiquity was produced early in small communities of farmers. The increasingly widespread use of the potter's wheel from about 3000 B.C. encouraged standardized mass-production; inventiveness and ingenuity of form and decoration then became much less

50. Parthian silver-gilt bowl from Iran, c. A.D. 100–200 (Dia. 11.6 cm.; 1976.76).

common. The prehistoric painted pottery from sites of the Hacilar culture in Turkey (pl. 15), of the Halaf Period in Mesopotamia and Syria, and of early village communities in Iran, hand-made and vigorously decorated, includes many ceramic masterpieces.

The production and manipulation of the *primary metals*, copper and lead, gold and silver, had been widely adopted by the later fourth millennium B.C. By the time of the famous "royal cemetery" at Ur, c. 2500 B.C. (pl. 22), all the basic techniques for the production and decoration of tools and weapons, personal ornaments and vessels, had been fully mastered in major urban centres in Sumer, often to an astonishing degree of excellence. Monumental work in metal rarely survives; but small-scale statuary cast in metal and such individual masterpieces as the head of an Akkadian king, c. 2300–2200 B.C., found at Nineveh in Iraq, illustrate remarkable skill with large-scale casting in copper or arsenical copper. Bronze, an alloy of copper and tin, was increasingly used from the mid-third millennium; but was always somewhat restricted by the distance (?Afghanistan) whence tin had to come.

Some iron had been produced as a by-product of copper smelting since late prehistory, notably in Turkey, but systematic exploitation of widely available *iron-ores* and the development of an appropriate iron technology to compete with bronze in efficiency only followed a complex and still little-understood series of changes in base metal supply and distribution, c. 1200–1000 B.C. Even then iron could not be cast, so copper and bronze endured as the media for a wide range of fittings, large and small, particularly where

decoration or rapid mass production, as with arrowheads, was vital. Initially iron's primary impact was on agricultural tools and the cutting edge of weapons. *Brass*, an alloy of copper and zinc, first appeared in restricted use in the mid-first millennium B.C. in Turkey.

Organic materials rarely survive, but the craft of carving *ivory* (both hippopotamus and elephant) is archaeologically evident from the fourth millennium B.C. In Bronze Age Canaan, and particularly in Iron Age Phoenicia and Syria, carved ivory was used for ornamental vessels and for decorating wooden furniture. The most famous survivors of this craft are numerous fragments from Assyrian palaces ("Nimrud Ivories") illustrating both the carved (and sometimes inlaid) styles of Phoenician and Syrian craftsmen (pl. 35) and the incised linear style native to Assyria itself between the ninth and seventh centuries B.C.

The sharp eye and creative impulse of ancient Near Eastern craftsmen survives most effectively today not in their treatment of inanimate or human subjects, but in their rendering of animals and zoomorphic detail. Animal-shaped amulets and weights of every kind, carved from stone, modelled in clay, or cast in metal, often vibrate with life and character wholly absent from surviving human sculpture. Pottery in animal forms or bronze objects with zoomorphic decoration, notably from Iran, survive to remind us, as does so much of the region's literary and religious legacy, that the special achievements of a people are as much to be found in the simpler things with which craftsmen embellish their own lives as in the commissions they executed for rich patrons in palaces and temples. This is fortunate, since it is the more mundane things, above all, that find their way into museum cases.

Concise Topographical Index of Excavated
Material from the Near East in the
Ashmolean Museum

('Tell', 'Tepe', etc. are ignored in the alphabetical sequence).

Abu Hurerya, Syria (Moore, 1972–1973)
Abu Shahrein, Iraq (Eridu) (Campbell-Thompson, 1918)
Tell Ajjul, Israel (Petrie, 1930–1934)
Al Mina, Turkey (Woolley, 1936–1937)
Tell Atchana, Turkey (Woolley, 1936–1939; 1946–1949)
Arpachiyah, Iraq (Mallowan, 1933)
Baba Jan Tepe, Iran (Goff, 1966–1969)
Bampur, Iran (de Cardi, 1966)
Barguthiat, Iraq (Watelin, 1933)
★Barlekin, Iran (Burton-Brown, 1956)
★Beycesultan, Turkey (Lloyd and Mellaart, 1954–1959)
Black Desert Survey, Jordan (Betts, 1981–1983)
Brak, Syria (Mallowan, 1937–1938)
Buseirah, Jordan (Bennett, 1971–1974)
Chagar Bazar, Syria (Mallowan, 1934–1937)
Choga Mami, Iraq (J. Oates, 1967)
Dhuweila, Jordan (Betts, 1986)
Tell ed-Duweir, Israel (Lachish) (Starkey, 1932–1938)
Eridu, Iraq (see Abu Shahrein)
Tell Farah (South), Israel (Petrie, 1928–1930)
Geoy Tepe, Iran (Burton-Brown, 1948)
★Hacilar, Turkey (Mellaart, 1957–1960)
Haftavan Tepe, Iran (Burney, 1968–1978)
Tell el-Hesi, Israel (Petrie and Bliss, 1890–1892)
Hissarlik (see Troy)
Hureidha, Yemen (Caton-Thompson, 1938)
Ingharra, Iraq (Kish) (Langdon, Mackay, Watelin, 1923–1933)
Jamdat Nasr, Iraq (Mackay and Watelin, 1925–1926, 1928)
Jawa, Jordan (Helms, 1972–1976)
Tell Jemmeh, Israel (Petrie, 1926–1927)
Jericho, West Bank Territories (Garstang, 1930–1936; Kenyon, 1952–1958)
Jerusalem (Kenyon, 1961–1967)

★Kara Tepe, Iran (Burton-Brown, 1956)
Kish, Iraq (see Ingharra and Uhaimir)
★Mersin, Turkey (Garstang, 1938–1940; 1946–1947)
Nimrud, Iraq (Mallowan and Oates, 1949–1962)
Nineveh, Iraq (Campbell-Thompson, 1927–1932)
Tall-i Nokhodi, Iran (Goff, 1961–1962)
Tepe Nush-i Jan, Iran (Stronach, 1967–1977)
Pasargadae, Iran (Stronach, 1961–1963)
Petra, Jordan (Parr, 1958–1964)
Tell Rimah, Iraq (Oates, 1964–1971)
★Samarra, Iraq (Herzfeld, 1911)
Susa, Iran (Louvre Loan)
Tell Taya, Iraq (Reade, 1967–1973)
Tawilan, Jordan (Bennett, 1968–1970; 1982)
Troy, Turkey (Schliemann, 1870–1890)
Uhaimir, Iraq (Kish) (Langdon and Mackay, 1923–1924)
Umm el-Biyara, Jordan (Bennett, 1960–1965)
Umm el-Jir, Iraq (Watelin, 1932)
Ur, Iraq (Woolley, 1922–1934)
Wadi Gazzeh, Israel (Macdonald, 1929–1930)
Yanik Tepe, Iran (Burney, 1960–1962)
Yarim Tepe, Iran (Stronach, 1960)

NOTES

1. An asterisk indicates only sherds.

2. A large collection of objects rescued by Woolley from clandestine excavations *in the vicinity of Carchemish* in 1913 is not listed above.

3. Finds from *Hira*, Iraq (Talbot Rice and Reitlinger, 1931) are held in the Department of Eastern Art.

Concise Bibliography

Background and General Studies

The Cambridge Ancient History (New Edition) (from 1970; these volumes contain extensive bibliographies).

W. C. Brice (ed.), *The Environmental History of the Near East since the Last Ice Age* (Academic Press, 1978).

S. Dalley, *Myths from Mesopotamia: Creation, the Flood, Gilgamesh and Others* (Oxford, 1989).

H. Frankfort, *The Art and Architecture of the Ancient Orient* (fourth revised impression, 1980).

S. Lloyd, *The Art of the Ancient Near East* (London, 1961).

—— *Mounds of the Ancient Near East* (Edinburgh, 1963).

—— *Foundations in the Dust* (2nd edition; London, 1980).

A. B. Knapp, *The History and Culture of Ancient Western Asia and Egypt* (Chicago, 1988).

C. K. Maisels, *The Emergence of Civilisation: from hunting and gathering to agriculture, cities, and the state in the Near East* (London and New York, 1990).

H. J. Nissen, *The Early History of the Ancient Near East, 9000–2000 B.C.* (Chicago, 1988).

M. V. Pope, *The Story of Decipherment* (London, 1975).

N. Postgate, *The First Empires* (Elsevier: Phaidon, 1977).

J. B. Pritchard (ed.), *Ancient Near Eastern Texts relating to the Old Testament* (third edition; Princeton, 1969). This volume includes translations of varied texts from all the major ancient languages of the Near East.

M. Roaf, *Cultural Atlas of Mesopotamia and the Ancient Near East* (Facts on file; New York and Oxford, 1990).

Prehistory

J. Mellaart, *The Neolithic of the Near East* (London, 1975).

—— *Catal Hüyük: A Neolithic Town in Anatolia* (London, 1967).

D. & J. Oates, *The Rise of Civilization* (Elsevier: Phaidon, 1976).

Regional: People and Places

A. Mazar, *Archaeology of the Land of the Bible, 10,000–586 B.C.E.* (The Anchor Bible Reference Library, Doubleday, 1990).

C. Burney and D. M. Lang, *The Peoples of the Hills: Ancient Ararat and Caucasus* (London, 1971).

H. Crawford, *Sumer and the Sumerians* (Cambridge, 1991).

S. Dalley, *Mari and Karana: Two Old Babylonian Cities* (London, 1984).

B. Doe, *Southern Arabia* (London, 1971).

R. N. Frye, *The Heritage of Persia* (2nd edition; London, 1976).

O. R. Gurney, *The Hittites* (Revised edition, 1980; Penguin Books).

W. Hinz, *The Lost World of Elam* (London, 1972).

D. B. Harden, *The Phoenicians* (Revised edition, London, 1986).

S. Lloyd, *The Archaeology of Mesopotamia* (London, 1978).

J. G. Macqueen, *The Hittites and their Contemporaries in Asia Minor* (Revised edition, London, 1986).

P. R. S. Moorey, *Biblical Lands* (New Edition; New York, 1991).

—— *Excavation in Palestine* (Lutterworth Press, 1981).

J. Oates, *Babylon* (Revised edition, London, 1986).

A. L. Oppenheim, *Ancient Mesopotamia: Portrait of a Civilization* (Revised edition, Chicago, 1977).

—— *Letters from Mesopotamia* (Chicago, 1968).

E. Porada, *Ancient Iran: The Art of Pre-Islamic Times* (London, 1965).

J. N. Postgate, *Early Mesopotamia: Society and Economy at the Dawn of History* (London & New York, 1992).

D. T. Potts, *The Arabian Gulf in Antiquity* (2 volumes, Oxford, 1990).

G. Roux, *Ancient Iraq* (2nd edition, 1980; Penguin Books).

The dissolution of the ancient Near East

R. Lane Fox, *Alexander the Great* (London, 1973).

The Ashmolean Near East Collections

B. Buchanan, *Catalogue of Ancient Near Eastern Seals in the Ashmolean Museum I: Cylinder Seals* (Oxford, 1966).

†B. Buchanan, edited by P. R. S. Moorey, *II: Prehistoric Stamp Seals* (Oxford, 1985).

†B. Buchanan and P. R. S. Moorey, *III: The Iron Age Stamp Seals c. 1200–350 B.C.* (Oxford, 1988).

P. R. S. Moorey, *Catalogue of the Ancient Persian Bronzes in the Ashmolean Museum* (Oxford, 1971).

—— *Kish Excavations 1923–1933* (with a microfiche catalogue of the objects in Oxford) (Oxford, 1978).

—— *Cemeteries of the First Millennium B.C. at Deve Hüyük* (B.A.R. International Series, 87, Oxford, 1980).

Acknowledgements

I am much indebted to Dr. Stephanie Dalley, Dr. Andrew Sherratt and Dr. Helen Whitehouse for their comments on a draft of this text. As I did not always take their advice, I alone am responsible for what survived. Charts I and II, particularly, owe much to their advice. Mr. N. R. Pollard undertook the photography and Mrs. Pat Jacobs the artwork. Mrs. Ruth Flanagan patiently typed my drafts. I am most grateful to them all. The photographs are reproduced by courtesy of the Visitors of the Ashmolean Museum.